Letting God Free Us

Letting God Free Us

Meditations on Ignatian Spiritual Exercises

Carlo Maria Martini

Foreword by George A. Maloney, S.J.

ST PAULS

Original title: *Mettere ordine nella propria vita*
©1992 Centro Ambrosiano, Edizioni Piemme
Translated by Richard Arnandez
Cover design: Sarah John

Scriptural quotations are from the
New American Bible with Revised New Testament
©1988 Glencoe Publishing Company

ST PAULS
Middlegreen, Slough SL3 6BT, United Kingdom
Moyglare Road, Maynooth, Co. Kildare, Ireland

English translation © ST PAULS 1993 and New City Press, NY 1993

ISBN 085439 452 4

Produced in the EEC
Printed by The Guernsey Press Co. Ltd., Guernsey, C.I.

ST PAULS is an activity of the priests and brothes of the Society of St Paul
who proclaim the Gospel through the media of social communication

Contents

Foreword 7
  Directed retreats — 8; A guided retreat — 9

Introduction 11
  Foreword — 11; Purpose and dynamism of the Exercises — 12;
  The Annotations in Ignatius' book — 14; The first Annotation —
  14; Annotation #15 — 17; Conclusion — 18

First Principle and Foundation (#23) 20
  The grace of adaptability and joy — 20; Analysis of #23 in the
  context of the Exercises — 23; Analysis of the text in the light of
  Ignatius' *Autobiography* — 28; Suggestions for biblical readings
  — 29; The fruit to ask for — 32; Pastoral significance of #23 — 33

Joy and Plenitude of the Kingdom (Homily) 35
  Liturgical readings — 35; The goal of our faith — 36; The mysterious path of purification — 38

Meditation On the Three Sins (#s 45-54) 40
  Analysis of #s 45-54 in the context of the Exercises — 41; Sin in
  the *Autobiography* of Ignatius — 43; Fruit of the meditation on
  the three sins — 46; Bible reading — 47; Pastoral note — 49

Sin and Mercy (#s 55-61) 50
  Analysis of #s 55-61 of the Exercises — 50; Bible readings — 55;
  Pastoral reflection — 55

Guided By the Holy Spirit (Homily) 58
  The letter of Peter and the gospel of Mark — 58; Two starting
  points for meditation — 60

The Repetitions and Additions (#s 62-90) 61
  The importance of repetition — 61; How repetition works — 63;

The fruit (#63) — 64; Meditation on hell (#s 65-71) — 70; The utility of the Additions (#s 73-90) — 71; Conclusion: God is not afraid of sin — 73

In Secret Before God (Homily) 74

Penance in the heart — 74; Before God — 75

The King's Summons (#s 91-98) 78

The call of the earthly king — 78; Examination of #s 91-98 in the context of the Exercises — 78; The meaning and dynamism of the parable of the king — 81; A biblical reading: the call of Peter — 84; The colloquy (#98): the Jesus whom we are following — 85; Ignatius' testimony in his *Autobiography* — 88

Dynamics of Contemplation: On the Incarnation
(#s 101-09) 9ι

The contemplation of the mysteries in the Exercises — 91; Contemplation on the incarnation (#s 101-09) — 93; Dynamics of contemplation — 95; Pastoral reflections — 97; Personal reflection — 98

The Way of Humility (Homily) 101

The way of the Messiah — 101; The only true way of life — 102

The Two Positions in Contrast (#s 136-46) 105

The fourth day (#136) — 107; Existence as a conflict — 107; The two fundamental symbols (#s 140, 142, 315) — 109; Christ's missionary mandate (#146) — 111; Conclusion — 114

An Authentic Christian Humanism 115

The pathway of interior liberty (#s 175-88 and 230-37) — 116; An authentic Christian humanism — 118; The sufficient attitude and the optimum attitude for free choice (#s 165-68) — 122

Expressing the Gospel in Our Surroundings (Homily) . . 126

An example of prophetic denunciation — 126; Authentic religiosity and love of neighbor — 127

Foreword

There are more than 5.4 billion human beings living on the face of planet earth. Never have we seen in our human history so many persons, each made by God-Trinity in the divine image and likeness of God. But, alas, never have we seen in our hearts so much evil, crime, fear of nuclear destruction of our planet and of oppression and genocide of whole races of people by corrupt politicians. Yet the hearts of all persons cry out for Someone who will call us to come to him for he is meek and humble of heart. His yoke is easy and his burden is light (Mt 11:28).

God is doing a wonderful work throughout our land. He is pouring out his Spirit of love in a renewing of Christ's Church that is exciting to experience. One evident sign of the outpouring of Jesus' Spirit is the tremendous hunger and thirst among Christians of all Churches and of all walks of life for deeper prayer in a more intense, immediate experience of the indwelling Trinity.

Retreat houses all over America are continuously filled as weary pilgrims seek to go aside and rest a while with God. Our modern life is becoming so hectic, fast and furious in its pace, that we feel torn from our primal roots. As flotsam tossed to and fro on a stormy ocean, we bob up and down in a fast rip tide of activities that tire us out as we are carried farther away from the shore.

We need to enter into an aloneness with the Alone, with God himself, if we are to find any meaning in our human existence. This is not escapism or avoidance of our responsibility to serve others. It is a movement of the Spirit to contact God and to experience him as the beginning and the end of our lives. As a feverish person on a sick bed cries for water to slake a burning thirst, we crave the experience of God, who alone can give direction and purpose to our fragmented lives.

Directed retreats

Many such Christians have discovered how much spiritual direction in God's word can be received in a "directed" retreat. Usually this takes the form of an eight- or thirty-day retreat under the guidance of a spiritual director. Such a director becomes a channel for the retreatant to experience the saving power of Jesus Christ in his *kairos* action as Christ's mysteries are prayerfully experienced, not as past history, but as the retreatant's present and evolving life of decision before the Trinity.

It is not always possible to find both the time to make a full, directed retreat and to find a good director, who can skillfully and prayerfully guide a person on a one-to-one basis. The Holy Spirit cannot be limited in his riches by our own human contingencies. Ignatius knew this and encouraged retreatants who could not go through the complete Spiritual Exercises, to make an "adapted" retreat. Such a retreatant receives from a director the developments of certain meditations and considerations which are to be prayed over at home.

The publishers give us in this book *Letting God Free Us*, a meditation manual drawn from an actual five-day retreat based strictly on the key meditations of the Ignatian Exercises that Cardinal Carlo M. Martini gave to the bishops of the region of Lombard in Italy in March of 1992. A Jesuit for forty-eight years, and now the Cardinal of Milan, Martini is well known as a scripture scholar and for his retreats given primarily to priests, bishops and religious. Such retreats adhere to the Ignatian meditations of the Spiritual Exercises, but bring together not only the intense biblical expertise of

Cardinal Martini, but also his deep prayer life and great
familiarity with the Exercises.

A guided retreat

Cardinal Martini has published several other books from
his Ignatian retreats that are usually drawn from the material
recorded on audio-tapes and transcribed. Most of these
published books, as this present one, consist of notes drawn
from the recordings made during the actual retreats that
Cardinal Martini had given to various groups. However,
usually he does not have time amidst his pastoral ministries
to personally supervise and edit the notes.

Yet the material does not seem to suffer in the process
and it is to the great advantage of the reader to be exposed
to Cardinal Martini's depth of scriptural knowledge and
wisdom of the spiritual life. In this book the reader will be
invited to pray out the five-day retreat that consisted of two
main conferences drawn from the Ignatian Exercises plus an
extended homily that usually relates the readings of the day
to Ignatian themes.

Cardinal Martini's scope was primarily to preach a five-day
retreat to bishops of northern Italy. Nevertheless, all who
not only read this book, but more importantly pray it out as
an adapted form of their own retreat will find great value
from the guidance of the scriptural scholar Martini as he
takes them through his interpretation of the Spiritual Exercises. In this retreat he shows, besides his vast knowledge
of the Old and New Testaments, also his deep spiritual life
and his enthusiasm and in-depth knowledge of the texts of
the Ignatian meditations as he links them skillfully with the
Annotations given in the Exercises.

For those already familiar with the Ignatian Spiritual Exercises, the author develops the usual Ignatian themes around
the general theme *To Put One's Life in Order* (#21). The

author submits each conference and each comment on the Ignatian meditations rigorously to attain his scope, namely, to bring a person, already well matured in the spiritual life, to new impulses of inner, spiritual movements to discern God's graces and more freely to make choices always according to the praise and glory of God.

We find, therefore, the basic Ignatian considerations offered to the reader of this book: The First Principle and Foundation; meditations on the three sins, one's own personal sins and on hell; the King's call; contemplations on the incarnation and other considerations of the Second Week; the hidden and public life of Christ; the two standards and three classes of human beings to attain "passionate" indifference in order to make free choices to follow Christ, King and suffering servant, God's love enfleshed for us, by living an authentic Christian life in contemplating God Trinity's immanent presence as dynamic, transforming love for each human person in the created world in which one lives.

This book is a work of art that combines Cardinal Martini's expert knowledge of the texts of the Ignatian Exercises with examples he draws skillfully from scripture and often from the *Autobiography* of Ignatius himself.

For anyone truly desirous to advance in the spiritual life, here is a book of great service to return to scripture and to the insights of the great Christian mystics, as focused upon in the Spiritual Exercises of Ignatius of Loyola. May you, reader and person of prayer, find in this work how to move deeper into the heart-spirit level of consciousness in order "to put order in your life," truly a gift that comes about only through the Holy Spirit, who is helped in his sanctifying work by the expert guidance of spiritual mentors such as Cardinal Carlo M. Martini.

George A. Maloney, S.J.

Introduction

Purpose and Dynamism of Ignatius' Exercises

Foreword

In view of the fifth centenary of the birth of Ignatius of Loyola (1491-1991) and of the 450th anniversary of the founding of the Company of Jesus (1540), both of which were commemorated recently, I was asked to give the Spiritual Exercises, using the text of St. Ignatius.

I willingly acceded to this request; but I must confess that being asked to conduct them using the text of St. Ignatius was for me a surprise and something of a challenge. For some twenty years I had given up (not the spirit, of course, but the letter) of the little book by Ignatius. It happened that in 1972 I was called upon to give a retreat for priests in my diocese, and since I did not have much time to prepare, I took as my text the gospel of Mark. From that time on I did not come back to the original text written by Ignatius over four hundred years ago, because doing so would have seemed to me a historical anachronism. Thus, for twenty years I gave retreats inviting those present to meditate either on one of the four gospels, or on some biblical figure (Peter, Paul, Abraham, Moses, Samuel, David, Job, Jacob, etc.) in the spirit and the dynamism of the Exercises, but without referring in any way to the contents of the book.

This time, however, having to deal with experienced and mature retreatants, I think that I can venture to take up again the original text in its own words, so that we may let ourselves be inspired in opening ourselves to God, in allowing ourselves to be found by him. In fact, for the next few days our basic occupation, beyond the meditations set before us, will be to let ourselves be found, in peace, by him who seeks us incessantly, and who, most especially, wishes to find us in this retreat.

Thanks be to you, O Lord, because you have called us together, relieving us of our usual occupations, often so weighty and demanding, because you wish to meet with us in peace. Dispose our hearts in peace and humility so that we may be found by you, responding to your insatiable desire to touch everyone's heart, life, existence and spirit, immediately, profoundly and gently.

Purpose and dynamism of the Exercises

Opening oneself to God is fundamental, given that the Exercises even in their most classical form as in Ignatius' book, proceed on two levels of development.

One level is more particularly ascetical; it seeks to put the retreatant in a position where he or she can make a decisive choice with liberty of heart and with an evangelical mind. This is the level clearly indicated in the title of the Ignatian text: "Spiritual Exercises to master oneself and to order one's own life without making decisions based on disorderly tendencies" (#21). "To order one's own life" does not simply mean to go to confession. It means to discover that order which is a qualifying choice of life according to God. Seeking to translate this title in a more positive way, we might say: "Spiritual exercises in view of making an important decision which will bring order into one's life, overcoming worldly influences, and setting aside disordinate affections." Such is the purpose of the Exercises.

Besides the level of ascetical development there is also a mystical level which is deeply imbedded in the Exercises, and is, as it were, their substance, their marrow, their secret and necessary sap. This level consists in experiencing directly the embrace of the mystery of God, the immediate contact with him, by letting oneself be touched by him. The mystical level underlies the Exercises from the very beginning; it is like a postulate, real but implied, in all that follows.

In this connection I find it useful to quote some words of Karl Rahner, taken from an essay written in 1978 and entitled: "Words of Ignatius of Loyola to a modern Jesuit." At one point Rahner has Ignatius say: "The main task incumbent on you Jesuits, and around which all else revolves, should be the preaching of the Spiritual Exercises to others. . . . You should understand all your other activities as a preparation for or a consequence of the ultimate task which awaits you in the future. That is, helping others to experience God directly, to discover that the incomprehensible mystery which we call God is near. And also that we can speak to him, that he makes us personally blessed if we do not seek to submit him to ourselves, but entrust ourselves unconditionally to him" (*Ignazio di Loyola,* Edizione Paoline, Rome, 1979).

This mystical level explains the deep dynamism of the Exercises as a whole, beyond that mere specific dynamism arising from the reflections and reasoning which lead to the choice of a state in life. Ignatius asks the exercitant to open himself or herself unconditionally to God's presence, and to the immediate experience of him.

If, then, the purpose of the process of these retreat days is to open oneself to the experience of God, the use of one or another text helps or hinders only so much. For this reason I shall confidently take up the original text of the Exercises as a point of reference.

The Annotations in Ignatius' book

Ignatius prefaces the actual Exercises with twenty Annotations. We find them entitled at the beginning of the book: "Annotations for giving some idea of the Spiritual Exercises which follow, and for helping both the one who gives them and the exercitant."

In Annotation #1 he explains what is meant by the word "exercises." In the others we find indications and suggestions addressed to exercitants (how they should act, how they should foresee their attitude and their reactions to what they will encounter further on) and to the director of the Exercises. For instance, "If the one who is presenting the Exercises notices that the exercitant in his or her soul is not receiving any spiritual experience such as consolation or desolation . . . he should question him or her" (#6). The indications for both parties are mingled because the experience of the two is closely connected.

As an introduction to the meditations, I advise you to read calmly Annotations #s 1, 2, 3, 5, 12, 13, 16, because these will help you to enter into the atmosphere suggested by Ignatius. Read them, asking yourself: What do these ancient words have to say to me as a praying believer? And again, what do they mean to me as a pastor of souls? These Annotations contain much pedagogical and pastoral wisdom, self-evident and hence important, even if, unfortunately, they are often overlooked in ordinary pastoral activity.

The first Annotation

Let us reflect together on Annotation #1, because it makes us understand what the Exercises are in their classical structure.

"By Spiritual Exercises we mean all forms of examination

of conscience, meditation, contemplation, vocal or mental prayer, or other spiritual activity, as we shall make clear farther on. In fact, just as walking, running, marching are corporal exercises, so we call spiritual exercises the various manners of preparing the soul and of disposing it to free itself from all disorderly affections, and, after having eliminated these, to seek and discover the will of God in the disposition of one's life, in view of saving one's soul."

This Annotation contains two parts. In the first four lines the Exercises are described as a series of spiritual activities. We do not *make* the Exercises if we do not devote our time to such endeavors as: the examination of conscience, meditation, contemplation, vocal and mental prayer as well as other spiritual activities. Let us note right away that we find here no mention of listening to sermons: no doubt it is understood that whoever gives the retreat speaks and explains a text; but to do the Exercises does not mean merely sitting and listening.

The second part of the Annotation tells us the purpose at which these exercises aim: it is something like physical exercise—walking, running, marching. The comparison is interesting. *Watching* a footrace or a wrestling match is not corporal exercise; one must actually take part personally in this activity. And what is the purpose of doing so? "We call spiritual exercises the various manners (in the Spanish it is more emphatic: 'every manner') of preparing and of disposing the soul."

Ignatius does not insist on the method he will propose; rather he stresses that any method is good. Hence there are infinite possibilities for applying these ideas outside of the letter of the Ignatian text. The important thing is that the soul should prepare and dispose itself "to rid itself of all disordinate affections . . ." This is the first characteristic which differentiates the Exercises from many other pious exercises of devotion and of contemplation which are also valid. Here we need to bring about the purification of the heart, to let God free us and purify us from our disordinate affections. It is God who works, thanks to that immediate contact which we mentioned above. Our task is to prepare and dispose ourselves to allow our hearts to be touched.

He goes on: ". . . and after eliminating these, to seek and find the will of God in the disposition of one's life, in view of the salvation of one's soul." If the first aim is purification, the second more specifically is to seek and to find the will of God, to encounter God who is calling us to follow him in the disposition of our lives, in our qualifying choices, in view of the salvation of my soul; hence in the perspective of eternity.

Thus, in synthesis, is the entire journey of the spiritual life: in the perspective of eternity, seeking what God wants of me, and seeking it in the conviction that I shall not find it if I do not dispose myself and allow myself to be interiorly and deeply purified.

The Spiritual Exercises came into being above all to prepare the exercitant to make a definitive choice, especially as regards his or her vocation for the kingdom of God, supposing that such choices for the kingdom are difficult and experience opposition, and come burdened with irksome conditions. Such is the hypothesis which we may characterize as the pessimistic one: There can be no choice for the kingdom that is not burdened with obstacles difficult to overcome. (For the persons whom Ignatius addressed, these might have been attachments to family, to money, to careers, to prestigious Court positions, etc.)

While the Exercises were conceived of as leading to life-determining choices, vocational choices which are made normally only once in a lifetime, they also touch the basic operations of moral living, of free choices according to the gospel. In this sense they affect many daily choices. If we examine ourselves as pastors, as men holding responsible positions in the Church, we realize that we are always confronted by the question: Is this choice which I am making or which I am urged to make, compatible with Christ? Is this disposition, this manner of leading the Church, of interpreting events, of expressing or not expressing myself, with reference to this or that situation, this choice which people expect of me, and which tradition seems to impose on me, truly evangelical? Is it the most adequate to reach the kingdom? Does it open the door to God's coming, or does it bar the gate to that power, impede or hamper its action?

The Exercises seek to help us respond to this fundamental challenge of the gospel, liberating us from all social, cultural and traditional conditioning, from the toils of spiritual blackmail, from the plea: "It has always been done this way"; from the laziness which can find entry even into the holiest places. The Exercises seek to help us to choose according to the gospel, and not according to what is most appealing, what best agrees with habit, with lack of imagination and creativity, with pastoral sloth; they seek to help us, not by offering us human norms of judgment (we already have enough of those) but by placing us before the purifying, attractive, overwhelming power of the Spirit, that is, in immediate contact with God.

Annotation #15

I should also like to read together with you a few lines from Annotation #15, where we clearly see that aspect of the Exercises which I have called mystical.

Here Ignatius develops an idea which we shall find again in the Exercises. During the retreat one should not bring pressure to bear on a person, pushing him or her toward one choice or another. Because, "during the Spiritual Exercises

in which we are seeking the will of God, it is more opportune, and much better, to let the Creator communicate
himself to the devout soul, drawing it in his love and to his
praise (the Spanish has: 'embracing it in his love and praise')
and guiding it in the path where it will best serve him in the
future."

This is the basic disposition for a choice: to prepare
oneself and dispose oneself for God's embrace, which draws
us to himself and makes us choose. And we must beg the
Lord for this grace because if it is not he who liberates and
guides us, our pastoral choices, both personal and spiritual,
will always be worldly, slothful and imperfect.

Conclusion

Considering Annotation #1 we have sought above all to
reflect on what the Exercises really are. Let us conclude this
introduction with two questions, which should give you
food for personal meditation:

— What am I asking for; what am I seeking in these days?

— How do I wish to dispose myself for God's action and
with what periods of personal involvement?

There are moments which are not part of the Exercises,
for example, times for listening; and there are provided
times which are part of the Exercises, for instance periods
of vocal prayer, and those given to the liturgy.

It is up to you to determine the time to be given to your
own meditation and contemplation, which Ignatius consid-
ers as true and genuine exercises (the others can be carried
out even during other moments). I therefore invite each one
to determine before God the hours and the moments to be
devoted to meditation. Ignatius insists that the exercitant,
once he or she has settled this, should not change the times
and not shorten the periods because of any aridity or weari-

ness. It is in fact especially in such moments that the Lord acts and communicates himself to us.

Help us, Lord, to dispose ourselves with an open soul for the grace of communication that you wish to give us, in these times so difficult for the Church and for humanity in its historic journey toward the fullness of your reign.

First Principle and Foundation
(#23)

The grace of adaptability and joy

What might be, for each one of us, the grace corresponding with the purpose of the Exercises, namely, seeking and finding in liberty of spirit the will of God in the disposition of our lives?

I thought of the grace of *adaptability* and *joy in our ecclesiastical ministry.* And so let us ask this of God in the name of our churches, of all our clergy, and of the entire praying community. It seems to me that this might indeed constitute a precious outcome of these days.

Let me comment briefly on such a grace.

Adaptability means knowing how to choose, once we have been freed from the bonds that weigh us down. I remember a dying priest friend who in the last moment of his agony repeated to me: "I offer which I suffer so that there may be more adaptability in the Church." He intended precisely that capacity of choosing freely, of considering events and situations with liberty and creativity, without fear of condemnations or criticism, and without letting oneself be influenced by such.

Joy is the opposite of the sense of oppression caused by the accumulation of things, even of pastoral duties, which we so often meet within our priests, and even in our own lives, while striving perhaps not to let this appear, so as not to aggravate others' burdens.

Sometimes the excess of initiatives, of proposals, of requests, of circulars, makes life in the presbyteries a heavy burden, and produces bewilderment in our clergy, confusion, a sense of anguish and weariness. And we don't manage to help them very much because we often have to ask them for even further efforts.

In his talk at the last synod Cardinal Ratzinger spoke with great understanding of the need for more simplicity, for higher holiness. At the same time he criticized the stifling weight of bureaucratic procedures in ecclesiastical administration. It is precisely in this situation of overwork, of overburdenedness, that the grace of adaptability and joy appears in all its importance. It is a grace of discernment, insofar as it helps us to select what is essential and to choose it, liberating us from the constraints of secondary things we may be attached to. This is, in fact, the grace that Jesus promised: "Come to me, all you who are heavy-burdened, and I will refresh you. Take up my yoke upon you and learn of me that I am gentle and humble of heart, and you will find rest for your souls; for my yoke is sweet and my burden light" (Mt 11:28-30).

We beg you, Lord, to reinvigorate our priests who are overburdened and weary, not by giving them easy solutions, but through a deep, supernatural intuition, by purifying them and enabling them to experience yourself. We pray to you for the priests overburdened by the weight of their ministry, by physical and psychological fatigue, by their years, so that they may come to realize, through interior purification and liberation that your yoke is sweet and your burden light. To all our clergy give the grace of adaptability and joy.

This is the grace to which Peter invites us in his first letter: "In this you rejoice, although now for a little while you may have to suffer through various trials, so that the genuineness of your faith, more precious than gold that is perishable, even though tested by fire, may prove to be for praise, glory and honor at the revelation of Jesus Christ. Although you have not seen him, you love him; even though you do not see him now, yet believe in him, you rejoice with an indescribable and glorious joy, as you attain the goal of your faith, the salvation of your souls" (1 Pt 1:6-9).

It is an unspeakable joy, which presupposes a long and courageous path of purification of the mind and which is, at the same time, a gift of God.

Preserving then, in our hearts, this grace which we wish to ask for, let us dwell for a moment on #23 of the Ignatian text which precedes the First Week of the Exercises. To explain it I thought it might be helpful to follow a method which takes into account five points which I shall make use of farther on as a source of successive reflections.

— First of all, I shall propose a very simple analysis of the text; this will be a rereading of the passage of Ignatius in the original context.

— I shall add, when I think it appropriate, a consideration from the *Autobiography*, a notable document for its spiritual richness, which is capable of shedding light on some passages of the Exercises.

— In the third place, we shall consider the fruit sought in the meditation. This is a very important factor in Ignatius' methodology; he wants us always to aim at a distinct fruit, and to ask for it as a gift.

— Then I shall indicate some possibilities for a renewed Bible reading, because Ignatius refers to holy scripture, and we too can do the same even more freely, considering the contemporary development of exegetical studies and the growth of knowledge of the Bible in the Church in the past four centuries.

— Finally I shall offer some suggestions for a pastoral rereading.

Analysis of #23 in the context of the Exercises

This #23 as we find it, under the title of "First Principle and Foundation," is not a meditation on which Ignatius invites us to dwell at length. In a certain sense it does not constitute part of the Exercises; it is a preliminary reflection and a logical postulate, in which the words "principle" and "foundation" are to be understood strictly in their Aristotelian meaning. Ignatius probably developed them in Paris, where for years he studied Aristotelian philosophy and, following the curriculum of the times, obtained doctorates in theology and philosophy, the top scientific degrees of the day.

"Principle," in the logical sense, indicates the basic truths on which a science is built. In themselves, these are not deductible or demonstrable. From these the other truths are derived. Aristotle, seeking to define the status of sciences, thought that every science arises from certain truths, which are its "principles" and which must be present in the entire successive progress of the science.

For this reason they are also the "foundation," that is, what is presupposed, built upon, and which is to be held as basic, remaining as implicit in the rest of the discussion.

Thus, Ignatius wishes to lay down, according to Aristotelian logic, a principle which we can always fall back upon, a principle which is obvious, which is evident, which goes without saying and does not demand laborious meditations. Such will come later on; yet still, in all the crucial moments of the process proposed by his text, implicitly or explicitly he will refer us back to these principles.

If we read the pages of his book carefully, we shall see that at the crucial points he brings us back to #23 in the form of implicit citations, which take up once more its essential terms. As we have already had occasion to remark, in Annotation #1 we find a reference to one of the key words of #23 (the salvation of one's soul) precisely because here we are dealing with a principle which is presupposed, with a fundamental principle.

But above all, in the central part of the Exercises where we find the rules for a good choice in life (cf. #s 169, 177, 179, 189), we hear a clear recall of the First Principle and Foundation, that is, of the fact that we are created to praise God and to save our souls. In fact, #169 states: "To make a good choice, insofar as it depends on me, my intention must be pure, and aimed solely at the end for which I was created, that is, the praise of God our Lord and the salvation of my soul." And in #177: "The third period is a period of tranquillity, when we consider above all the end for which we were born, namely, to praise God our Lord and to save our souls. Consequently, desiring this end, I shall choose as the means a state in life among those approved by the Church, so that I may be helped in serving the Lord and saving my own soul."

Thus, the principle is presupposed all along, and it is applied at the moment of the choice. We find it again in #179, where Ignatius carefully describes the method of making a good and valid decision: "I must keep in mind the end for which I was created, which is to praise God our Lord and save my soul; and at the same time I must remain indifferent, without any disordinate affections, so that I may not be inclined or eager to accept the thing proposed rather than to refuse it, or to refuse it rather than to accept it. Rather, I must keep myself in balance, like the weight on the lance of a scale, ready to perform what I shall judge most useful for the glory and praise of God our Lord, and for the salvation of my soul." In #189, suggesting the manner of reforming one's own life, Ignatius tells us how necessary it is to have a certain method, which will help us to "direct our existence and our state in life toward the glory and praise of God our Lord and toward the salvation of our own soul." At the end of this same #189 we read that, in distributing alms to the poor, or in dedicating ourselves to any good work, "we should not will anything else than to seek in all and for all the greater glory and praise of God our Lord."

If the purpose of the Exercises is to lead us to choices which correspond with the end of human existence and are therefore unaffected by worldly conditioning, #23 helps to clarify this purpose from the beginning.

Let us reread this page then, dividing it into its various parts, keeping in mind its importance for every human choice, and hence for uninhibited and joyful exercise of ecclesiastical ministry in the Church.

"We were created to praise, reverence and serve God our Lord, and thus to save our souls. Other things that exist in this world were created for us, to help us secure the end for which we were created. It follows that we must make use of them insofar as they help attain our end and must withdraw from them insofar as they are an obstacle to us. For this reason we must make ourselves indifferent with regard to all created things, in all that is left to the free choice of our will and is not forbidden. In such a way we will not desire health rather than illness; wealth rather than poverty; honor rather than dishonor; a long life rather than a short one; and so on for all the rest, desiring and choosing only what can lead us most surely to the end for which we were created" (#23).

This is a passage pregnant with meaning, probably composed by Ignatius little by little. He had a first, general intuition; and then he specified it better and better after reflections of an ethical nature. The text is also quite simplistic, because, wishing to bring together so many concepts, it states certain truths and alludes to many others. For instance, there is no christological reference here, but it is implied in the allusion to the mystery of God and of the soul's salvation. This page is not, therefore, a synthesis of theology or of the Christian life, but rather a summary of those axioms which must guide us along the path of the Exercises.

We can clearly subdivide this text into five parts:

— The general end of the created human being: to praise, reverence and serve God, and thus save one's own soul. This is the fundamental, substantive proposition.

— The end of other creatures: to help us achieve the purpose of our creation. This is the ethical theme of the relationship between end and means.

— The consequence which flows from the use of created realities according to their finality: We must make use of them insofar as they help us to reach our end and avoid them insofar as they constitute an obstacle.

— The necessity of interior liberty. This fourth part is a psychological consequence (the first being a theological affirmation; the second an affirmation of a rather more cosmological nature; the third, as we saw, an ethical consequence). It is necessary to make oneself indifferent toward all created things. The term "indifferent" in today's language no longer means what Ignatius meant by it, and it is preferable to translate it by the expression "interior liberty." We must enjoy interior liberty with regard to all existential situations, in particular all those specifically indicated in the paragraph: health or sickness, wealth or poverty, honor or dishonor, a long or a short life. For it is only by freely living these existential realities that we can attain our end. This fourth point is decisive for Ignatius, and the passage on the First Principle and Foundation really seeks to underline the supreme importance of this interior liberty, which is the aim of the Exercises, even if it is often presented as a meditation on creation.

— The fifth part sums up the whole matter: "to make properly oriented choices." It adds nothing new, but it surprises us by saying "desiring and choosing only what can lead us *most surely* to the end for which we were created." It repeats that we must be interiorly free to make a choice which will lead us to the end for which we were created. The impression of unexpectedness and the apparent incongruence in logic comes from what in Spanish is an adverb: *mas*, and which we translate here as "most surely" (or "best"). Where do these words come from? Obviously, if I want to attain an end, it is sufficient for me to use means which will enable me to do so certainly. The proportion means/end does not call for the *best* means. In reality, the adverb introduced here is highly important because it makes us grasp how, from the start of the Exercises, and even before entering upon the body of the Exercises themselves, the motive power of love is present, the urge to be *more* like Jesus. From this point the evangelical dynamism already begins to show itself. We are called not only to insure eternal life for ourselves through making proper choices—in us there is a motive force which impels us to make ourselves as far as possible like Jesus. So then, although veiled in a certain sort of formalism, and under an abstract guise, we find the tension which will ripple through every page of the Exercises.

For instance, in #97, in the third point of the meditation on the call of the eternal king, after stressing the importance of following a king who has an authentic mission and a great task to accomplish, we read that "those who wish to enlist *more* fully, and to distinguish themselves in every deed in the service of Jesus, their eternal king and universal Lord, will make an offering of *greater* value and *greater* importance." As we stand before Jesus the dynamism of the *tantum quantum* (I choose what is necessary to obtain my salvation) is replaced by the dynamism of evangelical love.

Again, in #109, at the colloquy of the meditation on the incarnation we ask the help of our "Mother and Queen so that we may follow and imitate our Lord *even more* closely."

From the very start Ignatius eagerly seeks to arouse this tension in the exercitant. On the other hand, the Exercises aim at a choice made according to the gospel, not one dictated by mere ethical rigor. They understand salvation as assimilation to Christ, as fullness of being with him, in a love which lets itself be transformed by the very love of Jesus.

In conclusion, #23 is indeed a bit stark and abstract; yet its implications are very rich.

Analysis of the text in the light of Ignatius' Autobiography

In the *Autobiography* of Ignatius we find references to #23. This work, dictated by the Saint and written in the third person, is very simple, very concrete, and hence it compensates for the abstract character found in #23. To quote a passage which can help us understand the mystical experience which lies behind the First Principle and Foundation I think it will be useful for us to reread the so-called "Vision on the Cardoner."

Ignatius describes the great graces he had received from the Lord at Manresa, and in #30 he speaks of the fifth of these: "On one occasion he went, out of devotion, to a church a little more than a mile from Manresa. I think it was dedicated to St. Paul. The road ran alongside a stream called the Cardoner. Entirely absorbed in his devotions he sat down for a moment, facing the torrent which was flowing down." (It is interesting to note the attention Ignatius pays to the posture of the body, and to the recollection which derives therefrom when its members are well positioned.) "While he remained seated there, the eyes of his intellect were opened; he did not have a vision, but he understood and grasped many principles of the interior life and many other things, both divine and human; all this appeared to him with so much clarity that it seemed to him entirely new. It is not possible to relate clearly the many truths which he then came to understand; all that can be said is that he received a strong intellectual light. His intellect was so intensely illuminated in this manner, that it seemed to him that he was a different man, or that his intellect had become different than it was before."

The extraordinary density of this passage may explain that intuition of the mystery of God as the end of human existence, and that dynamic turning to God of all one's actions, to which allusion is made in #23, and which will be developed in the course of the Exercises.

Suggestions for biblical readings

Before speaking of the fruit to be derived from our reflections on #23, I think it opportune to ask ourselves what biblical passages can be called to mind, because the language of holy scripture is familiar to us and is always very rich in meaning.

At once there comes to mind the passage in the Letter to the Ephesians, where Paul lays out the divine plan of salvation with a completeness and a charm far surpassing the rather abstract text of Ignatius. It will certainly be profitable to us to meditate on the words of the apostle, to revisit some of the truths contained in #23. This page from the Letter to the Ephesians (1:3-14) is deeply and clearly christological and trinitarian; it points out gloriously the end of humanity and of history; the recapitulation in Christ of all things. (Ignatius will speak explicitly of this only in the Second Week, for instance in the meditation on the kingdom.)

However, we do not find in Paul's passage the theme of choices regarding the things of this world, of their functionality, and of the need for interior liberty and purification. Though the Pauline passage gives us a fine commentary on the first and the second parts of the First Principle and Foundation it does not allude to the ideas contained in the third and fourth parts which are fundamental for Ignatius; hence we cannot consider it a parallel to #23.

So I thought of a few short biblical passages which speak directly about interior liberty. The most important of these is this from the Letter to the Romans:

"I urge you, therefore, brothers, by the mercies of God to offer your bodies as a living sacrifice, holy and pleasing to God; this is your spiritual worship. Do not conform yourself to this age but be transformed by the renewal of your mind, that you may discern what is the will of God, what is good and pleasing and perfect" (12:1-2).

Therefore, we are created to give praise and glory to God, to be a living sacrifice, holy and pleasing to the Lord. At the same time Paul insists, like Ignatius, on the fact that to attain our end, to be indeed a living sacrifice, holy and pleasing to God, we must free ourselves from the mentality of this world, and we must transform ourselves by renewing our minds, thus becoming capable of discerning what God wants. We are clearly in the Ignatian current. We must grasp among the realities of this world, among the possible choices open to us, among the various modalities of existence, what God really wants.

This same dynamism of choice is expressed in the Letter to the Philippians:

"And this is my prayer, that your love may increase ever more and more in knowledge and every kind of perception, to discern what is of value, so that you may be pure and blameless for the day of Christ, filled with the fruit of righteousness that comes through Jesus Christ for the glory and praise of God" (1:9-11).

This text tells us of the magnificence of the end (the glory and praise of God); such an end is to be attained in eternal life, in the salvation of our soul, in the day of Christ on which we must be found irreprehensible; but this is achieved only through the discernment which makes us distinguish what is best, and hence through a laborious task of purification.

A question may suddenly arise: Why should it be necessary to undergo so much labor of purification in order to know and to do the will of God? Why are we not able to achieve conformity with Christ save through a most wearisome process of interior purification? (As a rule, Christians think that it is enough not to commit any mortal sins in order to discover what God wishes; in reality, the path of spiritual asceticism is far more complex.) Why is it so difficult to achieve freedom in our existential choices which then remain, in fact, vitiated and imperfect?

Here we encounter the mystery of sin, of the historical weight of sin, of its incrustation in the individual and collective conscience; of its concretization in idols. We thus come into contact with the theme of sin as it pervades all the aspects and manifestations of human conscience.

We are confronted by a mystical vision of sin, like the one Ignatius must have seen near the Cardoner. It is not simply an ethical, pragmatic vision, which distinguishes good works from evil, but a vision that embraces us in our effort to free ourselves from the historical weight of social sin, and from all the conditions of fixedness that it takes on, be it in families, in society as a whole, in consciences, in habits, in fashions, in mentalities or in culture. Perhaps with the help of John of the Cross' "dark night," which is the logical unfolding of this idea of the Exercises, or, better still, through the personal experience of the "night of the spirit," the night of faith, one comes to understand to some extent the most wearisome path by which our most merciful and loving Lord purifies the soul in the course of a long and tortuous interior elaboration. It is then that one begins to glimpse the mysterious relationship that dominates human history. This is the relationship between God's mercy and human sin; mercy which changes into a purifying and relentless fire to make us fit to stand in God's presence and become irreprehensible on the day of Christ.

It is, then, the sight of the path leading toward full conformity with Christ, the Son of the Father which explains the necessity of purification in our daily choices. We are not dealing here with a reason proper to the ascetical order but rather with an intuition of the long, wearying pilgrimage to be accomplished in order to become sons and daughters in the Son. We detach ourselves along the way from the worldly conditioning which always pursues us, and weighs us down, and makes the majority of our concrete choices opaque and imperfect.

The fruit to ask for

The First Principle and Foundation is not really a meditation but a premise to be accepted, provided that it is based on a clear realization of God's lordship and of our creaturehood; of the transcendent, and of human existence. These days this realization is not at all obvious, and we can therefore ask for it as the practical fruit of rereading #23.

Obtain for us, O Lord, a deeper understanding of your sovereignty, of your supreme greatness, and of our creaturehood and our sinfulness. Give us the grace to experience that we are created by you, to know, love, and praise

*you; that we are nothing in your hands, and that you are
all for us.*

Pastoral significance of #23

We can gather the pastoral meaning or the First Principle
and Foundation as a reminder of our sense of creaturehood,
which today is so foreign to the mentality even of church-
going people. It is a deficiency which appears especially
when we are facing the great problems of the beginning and
of the ending of life (deciding for or against having children,
for or against euthanasia) or those referring to ecology and
the environment (people do not understand that we are not
the absolute masters of the garden but have been put in it to
cultivate it).

How can we promote this sense of creaturehood? How
can we help others to recover the sense of mystery, the
contemplative attitude, reverence for life, for our own being, for nature—a reverence which has nothing to do with a
kind of animism, but which enables us to see in all creation
a reflection of the mystery of God himself?

I often ask myself this question. I think that a simple and
practical way to help people immerse themselves in this
contemplative attitude is the habit of reverently listening to
the word of God, of God who disposes of us, so that our
happiness lies in abandoning ourselves into his hands; so
that we may allow ourselves to be nourished by his word of
life. Reading holy scripture even in short passages with a
eucharistic attitude is a most powerful antidote against the
profane spirit, because in the Bible God manifests himself to
us as Creator, Lord and Father.

I do not think that to bring people to this sense of being
created there is much to be gained from apologetic, or from
scientific reflections on the origin of the universe and of life.

We need to place ourselves before God, Creator, Lord and Father, brought vividly to us particularly when we lovingly listen to his written word.

The Lord will, no doubt, illuminate us on this point, which is one of the major problems of our pastoral function. On our side, let us seek to live as created beings, especially in an attitude of prayer. For this, I would like to end by rereading Annotations #3 and #5:

"When we speak, orally or mentally, with God our Lord and with his saints, greater respect is called for than when we make use of our intellect to understand" (#3). "It is very helpful for the one who is making the Exercises to enter upon them with great courage and a generous attitude toward his Creator and Lord, offering entirely to him his will and his liberty, so that the divine Majesty may make use of them according to his most holy will as regards himself and all he possesses" (#5).

The attitude of reverence and of respect, and the readiness to give, are two ways in which we can concretely express, even in our prayer, our sense of dependence on God by whom we are created, from whom we have received all, and from whom we expect all.

Joy and Plenitude
of the Kingdom

(Homily of Monday of the Eighth Week of the Year)

Liturgical readings

"Blessed be the God and Father of our Lord Jesus Christ, who in his great mercy gave us a new birth to a living hope through the resurrection of Jesus Christ from the dead, to an inheritance that is imperishable, undefiled and unfading, kept in heaven for you who by the power of God are safeguarded through faith to a salvation that is ready to be revealed in the final time. In this you rejoice, although now for a little while you may have to suffer through various trials, so that the genuineness of your faith, more precious than gold that is perishable even though tested by fire, may prove to be for praise, glory and honor at the revelation of Jesus Christ. Although you have not seen him you love him; even though you do not see him now, yet believe in him, you rejoice with an indescribable and glorious joy, as you attain the goal of your faith, the salvation of your souls" (1 Pt 1:3-9).

"As he was setting out on a journey a man ran up, knelt down before him, and asked him: 'Good teacher, what must I do to inherit eternal life?' Jesus answered him: 'Why do you call me good? No one is good but God alone. You know the commandments: "you shall not kill; you shall not commit adultery; you shall not steal; you shall not bear false witness; you shall not defraud; honor your father and your mother."'

"He replied and said to him: 'Teacher, all of these I have observed from my youth.' Jesus, looking at him, loved him and said to him: 'You are lacking in one thing. Go, sell what you have and give it to the poor, and you will have treasure in heaven: then come and follow me.' At that statement his face fell, and he went away sad, for he had many possessions" (Mk 10:17-27).

The goal of our faith

Note right away the connection between what the Exercises propose to us as the end of human existence, and what the apostle Peter describes as the synthesis of the believer's journey. The Exercises call for purification in view of making proper choices in accordance with God's plans, for the salvation of our souls. Peter speaks of the "goal of our faith" which is attained through trials.

The question put by the rich young man, as related by Mark, has to do with the theme of eternal life.

The background of the whole search is, therefore, our salvation, our eternal salvation. Faith itself is conceived of as a journey leading to that end. "You . . . are safeguarded through faith unto a salvation that is ready to be revealed in the final time." Eternal life, the goal of the entire journey, is called by Peter "a living hope, an incorruptible heritage, reserved in heaven for you."

We can find in these words what Ignatius proposes as the obvious conclusion of the Exercises, namely, the primacy of the end: all reality, all situations must be evaluated in their relationship with eternal life.

Four centuries ago, when Ignatius was alive, it was obvious to all that the end of human existence was salvation for eternity; naturally, there were those who did not think about this, or forgot about it, who lived as though eternity did not exist; but this truth was in some manner taken for granted; and whenever it was appealed to, nobody except a few rationalists or freethinkers had any objection to advance.

Today this awareness is often lacking among people, even good people. Mentalities have changed profoundly, and we must take this into account from the pastoral point of view. For that precise reason I thought, for instance, of concluding the diocese's series of pastoral projects on major ethical attitudes with a project on the theme of "being vigilant." To learn again how to look upon life in the light of eternity, how to wait for the Lord who is coming, is very important, because it touches a nodal point of the Christian understanding of existence. It is a point which is often soft-pedaled, which remains within parentheses and, while not being openly denied, is not at all determining or decisive in our day-to-day choices.

It can happen even in the life of a bishop, who certainly feels the transitoriness of everything he does, to be so overburdened with problems, with vital and urgent questions, that he may run the risk of forgetting that only the final goal, salvation "ready to be revealed in the final time," is what gives importance to everything else. We must beg the Lord, therefore, to stir up again in us the certainty of this perspective which fills us with joy. Our very afflictions are a cause of joy, because they are a sign of that transitoriness. "In this you rejoice, although now for a little while you may have to suffer through various trials." We reach our goal after a journey of purification, and our trials confirm that this purification is truly taking place. For this reason they afford us joy, making us tangibly aware that God loves us and is preparing us for such a tremendous goal.

Joy should be the special characteristic in the lives of us bishops, of us who are called to teach others the relative value of so many things. When, for instance, we note how political passions, quarrels and the various forms of exasperation thrive all around us, can we put all this into proper perspective, thanks to the joy that belongs to people who keep thinking of the goal of life? Do we live our trials as tests which demonstrate the truth of our faith and as signs that the Lord is purifying us? This conviction lies at the root of the entire journey of the Exercises, because we cannot make valid choices if we do not let ourselves be consumed in the fire of suffering, a fire that then is changed into the "praise, glory and honor of the manifestation of Jesus Christ."

The mysterious path of purification

Of the gospel passage I should like to stress a single aspect. The young man seems to be ready to refuse something which in itself is not obligatory. "If you *want* to be perfect, go, sell what you have and give it to the poor, and you will have treasure in heaven: then come and follow me."

It would seem that not everyone is called to this kind of discipleship and that observing the commandments is enough.

Yet, after the rich young man had refused the invitation, Jesus deplores the obstacle that wealth presents for entering into the kingdom. "How difficult it is for those who are rich to enter the kingdom of heaven!"

Let us then try to understand the difference between using goods according to God's commandments (as the young man who came to Jesus had already done), and undertaking a more perfect pursuit of the end, which is required of us by the dynamism of the kingdom. It is difficult to serve God with a pure heart when we possess riches, not only of a material kind, but human, spiritual, cultural, ecclesiastical riches as well, because they entangle us, preventing us, as we shall see, from enjoying the liberty of choice we need if we are to follow Christ aright. This is true even when we are dealing with riches which are good, like those mentioned by the young man; even when they involve my personal prestige, my good name, my reputation. The answer Jesus gave was so strong that the disciples remained amazed; so at first he repeats what he had said, but then injects into the discussion an element of hope: "What is impossible for men is possible for God, because for God all things are possible." In this way he points out the gospel course, the path of purification through seeking the will of God, which is open to all.

Give us, O Lord, you who are present in this eucharist which we are celebrating, the grace to understand the mystery of this path which, through delivering us from attachment to values, situations, and realities even when these are good, may bring us to the joy and the plenitude of following you into your kingdom.

Meditation On the Three Sins
(#s 45-54)

We have seen that the First Principle and Foundation is entirely oriented toward the end: we are created to praise, reverence and serve God. Other realities are created for us, to help us attain our end; we must choose what can best lead us to our end, and this end is our salvation.

This salvation, however, considered in a trinitarian perspective (from the Father, in the Son, and by the mediation of the Holy Spirit) and from a Christian point of view (salvation through assimilation to Jesus Christ), is not simply a question of saving ourselves from hell but of being with the Son, making ourselves like him and abiding in him.

Indeed, the fire of the Father's infinite mercy moves us, follows us, devours us, transforms and transfigures us until we are like the Son. To resist this transforming action is unhappiness, hell. On the contrary, if we allow ourselves to be loved, this transforming action of divine mercy becomes the gently purifying flame which delivers us from our personal, social, historical, hereditary and cultural imperfections. It makes us breathe freely in the atmosphere of liberty given us by Jesus the Son, who, in his love for us, went ahead through the purifying fires of death, just as he went down into the waters of baptism, in order to redeem us from our sins and call us to join him in his march into glory.

In the light of the purifying mercy of the Father and of the Son, by the grace of the Spirit, let us reread the first true meditation of the First Week of the Exercises, also called the meditation "on the three sins" (#s 45-54).

We begin with sins, because in fact this is the actual start of the historical pathway of purification for anyone who wants to conform himself to Jesus Christ. From this point Jesus begins his preaching ("Be converted, and believe the

40

gospel," Mk 1:15) as does Peter's message ("You must reform and be baptized, each one of you, in the name of Jesus
Christ, that your sins may be forgiven," Acts 2:38). This
meditation of Ignatius is a long, ample, and dense study of
the matter. I shall call attention only to certain aspects
thereof, following the five points previously indicated:

— Examination of the passage in the context of the whole
book.

— Reflection on the *Autobiography* of Ignatius, to understand how he personally lived the sense of sin and of conversion which he afterwards expressed in this First Week.

— Question the fruit, or one of the fruits, of this meditation
which offers great richness and which remains as a permanent background to Christian life.

— Suggested Bible readings.

— Some specifically pastoral considerations.

Analysis of #s 45-54 in the context of the Exercises

Let me at once point out that the text which each one of
you will reread, comes to us with a fragrance of times past;
four centuries of research in theology and of ecclesiastical
reflections do not go by in vain. However, this distance
allows us to understand better what is valid and substantial
in these pages.

We begin with #45, which expresses in very precise
language the method, the matter and the material of this
meditation. "First exercise: meditation on the first, the second and the third sin, using the three faculties of the soul.
After a preparatory prayer and two preludes, there follow
three principal points and a colloquy." Ignatius reminds us
that here we are beginning to exercise ourselves by remembering, by reflecting, and by praying.

His *method* is that of meditating: reasoning and prolonged reflections using the three faculties of the soul, memory, intellect and will (borrowed from Aristotelian psychology and metaphysics, but possessing great pedagogical value). The meditation includes "after a preparatory prayer and two preludes, three main points and a colloquy."

Interesting is the attention paid to the passages, to the details, so that the exercitant may see clearly how he or she should proceed, and with what pedagogical plans he or she must enter upon this meditation.

The *matter* or the theme is made up of the first, the second and the third sin. The enumeration is simple and easy to remember and is concretely expressed in the first sin that can be recalled in salvation history (the sin of the angels); in the second sin (that of Adam and Eve); and in the third, that of a sinner who, for a single mortal sin has fallen into hell.

The *material* for this meditation is drawn from holy scripture, in particular Genesis 3, as regards the second sin, and from patristic and theological tradition as regards the sin of the angels as well as the hypothesis of a person condemned to hell for a single mortal sin.

All this is presented in a very incisive way, without all the theological subtleties which we are used to when examining such questions. Hence, as we consider this text, we might be disturbed by questions such as: What, really, was the sin of the angels? What are the demons? Is it possible for anyone to be damned for a single mortal sin? In Ignatius' world, a world much simpler than our own and more familiar with the fear of God, such questions simply did not arise.

It still remains a meaningful and important passage, to such an extent that Ignatius repeats it twice in the same day; he gives us five meditations per day: the first (which we are considering now) is on the three sins; the second on our own sins; the third is a repetition of the first two; the fourth a repetition of the third; and the fifth a meditation on hell.

I leave to you to read #s 45-54 and wish to emphasize #53, the final colloquy, which is a decisive page in the remaining steps on the path of purification, of self-offering, and of following Christ. "I shall imagine Christ our Lord hanging on the cross before me, and I shall speak with him: He the Creator became a man, and from the abode of eternal life he has come down to die a temporal death for my sins. I shall likewise examine myself: What have I done for Christ? What am I doing for Christ? What should I do for Christ? Finally, beholding him in that state, hanging on the cross, I shall express those sentiments which will arise in my heart." This is the only part of the whole text which remains implied even in the successive weeks of the Exercises. The fundamental attitudes remain: I am a forgiven sinner because if I am here now I owe it to Jesus, to his cross, to his limitless love. Beholding him I know that I owe him everything; because of this, every desire he has concerning me is for me an order; I owe him full trust, given that he saved me from total ruin.

Such sentiments of generosity, dedication, trust, eagerness in following Jesus, are the fruits which we shall find again in the rest of the book and in Christian life.

Sin in the Autobiography *of Ignatius*

For now, however, I am anxious to ask myself along with you what we should retain from the pages which precede this #53, the meditation on sins and on human disorder.

It may help us to find an answer if we examine Ignatius' own experience as described in his *Autobiography*. In truth, there are few mentions of the theme of sin in the story of his life, which brought him from a worldly existence to the conversion at Manresa, then to Jerusalem, and finally to Rome. (Jerusalem holds a central position in the whole

Autobiography, and Ignatius would have wished to remain there. Since this was not possible, he transformed his ideal in service of the Church of Rome.)

We find the first mention of sin at the very start of the book:

"Until the age of twenty-six, he was a man of the world, absorbed by its vanities. He especially liked to practice the use of arms, being led on by an immense desire to gain vain honor" (#1). Here, sin is presented under the guise of worldliness and vanity. Ignatius tells us little about his existence during his first twenty-six years, but this must obviously have been a rather free-ranging period in his life. On the occasion of the Ignatian centenary, mention was even made of an illegitimate daughter of his. This detail was brought to light after the discovery of certain documents which probably had been deliberately sidetracked by the early Jesuits. However, one passage in the *Autobiography* may allude directly to this matter. After his conversion he went on a trip to collect from the Duke some money owed to him, "and once he had received this money he sent it to some persons toward whom he had certain obligations" (#13). Be that as it may, in his account Ignatius especially stresses the sins of vanity and ambition. And, as he says in the Exercises, from vanity and ambition all other vices spring.

He comes back to the vice of vanity in #6 when he tells us about the thoughts which tormented him during his illness. And in #10 there is an expression which gives us to understand how purification was for him a gift of God. "Holy desires went on, driving out the earlier thoughts." Purification did not come about only through the thought of the sins committed, but also through his flaming desires for the love of God. Then he describes a vision of our Lady with the child Jesus, which he contemplated at length, finding therein deep consolation. "There came over him such disgust for all his past life, especially as regards carnal failings, that it seemed to him that all the imaginations which previously had been so deeply rooted and vivid had disappeared from his soul. From that time [1521] to August 1553 in which this memorial is being written, he never gave even the least consent to sensual solicitations." Hence, I repeat, Ignatius considered the grace of repentance and of purification as a gift of God which changed his entire existence.

The idea of sin returns a few more times, but it is interesting to note that it returns along with the desire to please God. (This is the moving force of the colloquy in #53 of the Exercises.) "When he resolved to do severe penance, he was not so much concerned with making up for his sins, as with doing something pleasing and agreeable to God." And he adds: "He experienced a very great horror for the sins of his past life; but the desire to perform great things for the service of God was so powerful that, although not judging that his past sins were already pardoned, he did not think much of them during the penances he inflicted on himself" (#14).

However, although he was henceforth attracted solely by the need to give glory to God, in #17 he tells us about a general confession which lasted for three days, and this helps us to understand how attentively Ignatius went about purifying himself. Above all, he describes in #s 22-26 the purification that he went through because of scruples and the long, painful and almost despairing road which he had to traverse, allowing himself to be purified by God.

We find a final, conclusive and especially interesting allusion in #99, where he declares that "he had much offended our Lord after he had embraced his service, but he had never consented to a mortal sin; indeed, he had gone forward growing more and more in devotion, which means in the facility of finding God."

We might say that in the *Autobiography* the place held by sin is certainly important, but not preponderant; it is a memory of the past, but what counts is to work for the glory of God.

Fruit of the meditation on the three sins

What concrete fruit did Ignatius have in mind in this first meditation of the Exercises, besides the principal one, which is to stimulate generosity toward Jesus Christ?

I think that in his long description of the first, second and third sin there is a fruit to be considered, which has a permanent effect on Christian life: a correct understanding of sin, as seen before God, in his plans and in his light. This is especially important in our times.

Concretely, we should obtain from this meditation a realization of the dissemination of sin throughout history, a better grasp of how disobeying God by refusing this gift of sonship has consequences in heaven and on earth: in the angels in heaven, in the first human beings and in their posterity on earth, as well as in every individual human being who refuses divine sonship. We can say that as regards the religious aspect of our lives, sin determines a degeneration of our relationship with God on the one hand and among people on the other, resulting also in a degeneration of society, of history and of morals. Finally it brings about the degeneration of each individual.

So then, the reflections that Ignatius proposes for the meditation of the three sins help us grasp the dramatic disorder which follows our lack of submission to God, our disobedience, our refusal of creaturehood, our scorn for the gift of sonship; a disorder which pervades the world in its religious, civil, family and individual aspects. This theological and mystical vision of sin is, thank God, another gift of his. It is an outlook sorely needed today, especially for whoever as a pastor is called to understand the religious, historic, civil, social and personal disorder in which the salvific action of Christ and his Church has to operate.

Bible reading

It seems opportune to propose a biblical reading on the theme of the three sins, and Ignatius himself suggests it, referring to chapter 3 of Genesis.

However, wishing to widen his point of view, I invite you to reflect on chapters 3-11 of Genesis, in the light of the first two chapters, because these constitute the best actualization of Ignatius' text.

What do the first two chapters of Genesis show us? The beautiful spectacle of a triple relationship, the fecundity of a triple right order:

1) A relationship of filial dependence between Creator and created, humanity and God, which makes God look with complacency on us and converse with us. In this relationship we are not afraid of God nor do we tremble before him.

2) A proper, fruitful relationship between man and woman, made for each other, made to help each other; a relationship in which all relationships with others is foreshadowed, a relationship of complementarity between persons.

3) A proper relationship between humanity and nature, a nature that is friendly and an environment that is hospitable and not overwhelming. Work is the development of this relationship with the environment.

This is the way of life pointed out to the human being from the start: "Do this and you shall live."

From chapter 3 to chapter 11 instead, Genesis shows us the way of death, generated by the rupture of that triple harmony:

1) The relationship between God and humanity is destroyed; because of this Adam and Eve hide, are afraid of God; from this arise all the religious degenerations founded on fear of God.

2) The relationship between man and woman, between brothers and sisters is also ruined. Adam accuses Eve (Gn 3:10). Cain does not tolerate Abel's diversity, and kills him (Gn 4:8).

3) Subverted too is the relationship between humanity and nature: the flood (Gn 6-8); and between human beings and their environment: Babel (Gn 11), where we see that the construction of the city is not a factor of harmony but of division.

This is the path of death: the refusal of filial trust causes the degeneration of all the relationships which constitute us as persons in our relationship with God, with others and with nature.

It then becomes possible to read the three great patriarchal stories, from chapter 12 to the end of Genesis, as a laborious reconstruction of the bases of these three relationships:

1) The story of Abraham represents the toilsome rebuilding of the trusting relationship between humanity and God, founded on filial abandonment and total trust.

2) Jacob illustrates the painful restoration of fraternal relationships with Esau.

3) Joseph signifies the renewal of a correct relationship with earth: He is the one who not only reconciles the brothers to each other and to himself, but he knows how to administer with frugality and wisdom the goods of Egypt.

We can, therefore, enrich the first meditation of the Exercises with a biblical reflection on primitive history, to gather from it the sense of sin in God's plan, and consequently the pervasiveness of sin and the laborious rebuilding of God's way of life.

Pastoral note

Today we rightly lament the lack of a sense of sin in the world. But we must admit that, understood as a consciousness of disorder in our world, we do not lack this sense. People are seemingly more and more convinced that the world is going badly. We hear resounding denunciations of corruption in politics, of ecological disturbances, and of the wrongs done by rich countries to the poorer ones.

What is lacking is an understanding of the root of such disorders; the awareness that these evils are caused by opposition to love, to the divine plan, to distrust of God as our Father. What is lacking, and we shall see more of this later, is the realization of my own personal complicity in this distrust of God our Father; it is perceived as an objective disorder, for which the individual is not guilty.

I think that as pastors we are called to make clear the theological roots of the disorder existing in the world and to help people recognize it as a personal sin, as a sin each of us is guilty of. We are called to stress the cause of all this: the distrust of God our Father and loving Lord, of his plan of positive love, of his triple order of justice.

May the Lord give us that sense of sin and of mercy which will help us to feed the sheep always tempted to lose their way and to destroy themselves through want of trust in God. May he grant this to us and to all our people!

Sin and Mercy (#s 55-61)

The second meditation for the First Week of the Exercises is on sin (#s 55-61), i.e., on the consciousness that I too am responsible for the disorder present in the world, which flows from the refusal of divine sonship and of the Father's plan.

We read previously the passage in the *Autobiography* in which Ignatius confesses that "he had much offended our Lord, after he had embraced his service, but he had never consented to a mortal sin" (#99). This statement helps us to actualize the reflections we shall make today: What does it mean to have offended God much, while still serving him closely?

To reply to this question I shall dwell especially on the text; then I shall offer you a short biblical reading and a few reflections of a practical pastoral nature.

Analysis of #s 55-61 of the Exercises

The title recalls that of #45 and states: "Second exercise: a meditation on sin; after the preparatory prayer and the two preludes it includes five points and a colloquy. The preparatory prayer is the same" (#55).

Let me briefly comment on the expression used here, referring to #46, where it was said: "The preparatory prayer consists in asking God our Lord for the grace that all my intentions, activities and operations may tend solely to the service and praise of his divine Majesty."

It is noticeable that this formula, prefacing all the exercises of the entire four weeks, not only makes us ask that our meditation and prayer may proceed well, but also asks for the right orientation of all our actions (including prayer) so as to conform them with the purpose of every human activity, that is, with God's plan, according to the First Principle and Foundation. We are asking that the actions of our whole life may be dedicated exclusively to the service and praise of the Lord.

This impresses me, because it is a question of a grace, of a gift from on high. God is the source of my right thinking, right doing, right praying. Ignatius wants us to recognize before every meditation, that if everything we do is directed toward our end, it will be such only as a result of the Holy Spirit's action and gift.

Striking also is #58: "The second prelude consists in asking for what I want, namely, a deep and intense sorrow and tears for my sins."

This again is a gift, not something which can be forced. The mention of tears reminds us of a gift which Ignatius had received in abundance. This is made clear in his spiritual diary, those little notebooks where almost daily he notes "tears" as a characteristic of his mental prayer and his Mass. Ambrose speaks of tears as a fruit of grace several times, recalling his work as a confessor. He used to weep, especially when he heard the sins of those who came to confess to him. And Charles Borromeo is often represented in prayer, weeping and wiping away his tears.

Tears are therefore a gift which belongs to the Church's tradition, even though they seem rather outlandish to our way of thinking, which has so little regard for spiritual affectivity.

Let us now go on to the points of the meditation. The first

consists "in reviewing my sins. I should, in other words, call to mind all the sins of my life, examining them year by year, or period by period. In this connection, three considerations are useful: calling to mind the area and the house where I lived, the relationships which I had with others, and the activities I engaged in" (#56). He suggests that this review of our sins should be chronological (according to periods) and then considered according to circumstances (places, relationships, activities) so as to grasp better the disorder in my life, my lack of trustful response to God's plans for me. We must not merely meditate on the sins in themselves, but on our lack of personal correspondence with God's plan for us.

This examination should turn into a personal inquiry: What did God want to bring about through my existence? What did he want to do with me considering the law of life laid down in Genesis (1-2) and the programmatic passages of holy scripture such as the first chapter of the Letter to the Ephesians? What masterpiece can God not bring about because of my past and present resistance?

As for the circumstances (places, relationships, activities) we can say that the Lord wishes to sanctify through me the places and areas which I inhabit to irradiate them with his glory. He wishes, farther, to divinize the relationships that he gives me to develop, impregnating them with supernatural love, with the holy Spirit, with zeal and fire. He wants to transfigure my activities, making them resemble those of Jesus Christ. God wills effectively, lovingly, faithfully, that all the circumstances of my life should help me be a true son or daughter.

But I, what have I made of all this?

This review of sins suggested by Ignatius is a consideration of God's plan for me. A plan which he always had and still has, but which I have not carried out.

In the light of this premise, it is easier to understand the second point: "I must evaluate my sins, considering the ugliness and malice which every mortal sin we commit has by its very nature, even if it is not a question of things forbidden" (#57). There immediately comes to mind #99 of the *Autobiography:* Ignatius, after having dedicated himself to God's service, "had much offended our Lord," even though he never consented to a mortal sin.

The second point invites us to consider the ugliness and the malice of sin.

Ugliness is an esthetic notion. It is the distortion of my manner of being, compared to the esthetics of God's glory; the deformity of my life, compared with the glorious beauty of the divine plan which the Lord, relying on me, wishes to bring about. (You might want to reread the splendid pages of Hans Urs von Balthasar on glory, and on its repercussions in the cosmos as well as in history.)

Malice, on the other hand, is an ethical and personalistic concept; it is the mistrust of a son regarding the Father's merciful and saving design.

Ugliness and malice are resistance to the glory and the goodness of the divine action.

To bring #s 56-57 into relief concretely, we should read over our own list of responsibilities, beginning with our own true vocation, with what God truly calls us to be today, with that very special name which God gave us from all eternity in baptism. . . . I must begin, in other words, with my true identity as God intended it in his plan for me, part of which is the gift of my episcopal ministry—a call to my personal version of episcopal holiness in its historical uniqueness. I must consider my history of offending God, my distrust of his plan for me, my neglectfulness, my carelessness in grasping the significance of my life for the salvation of the whole world.

In this light, there can arise from the depths of my being intense sorrow and tears.

I shall not comment on #s 58-59 (the third and fourth

points). These propose a deep, affective reflection of an Augustinian type. On the double question, "Who is God, and who am I?" the contrast is outlined which makes it clear what it means not to respond to God's trust, to fail to correspond with his salvation plan. The texts may seem to us a bit rhetorical, but what we are trying to do is precisely to grasp the dynamism of spiritual affectivity.

From this there springs forth the fifth point: "A cry of stupor, with profound emotion, considering that all creatures have let me live on, and helped preserve my life; the angels who bear the sword of divine justice have supported me, preserved me and prayed for me. The saints have continued to intercede for me; heaven, the sun, the moon, the stars and the elements, the fruits, the birds, the fish and other animals . . . and the earth did not open to swallow me, creating new hells where I might be tormented for all eternity" (#60).

True, this cry of amazement smacks of rhetoric, but in the life of Ignatius and of other saints, this attitude is rather a mystical grace: understanding who God is, and who I am, feeling the dire need for his mercy and the thirst to glorify it precisely because of its prime importance for the rest of my existence.

In fact, the final colloquy brings out the infinite chasm between divine mercy, God's plan of love, and my own wretchedness, my coldness, infidelity, my lack of correspondence, the paltriness of my service of God, all of which are constantly enveloped in the unlimited mercy of the Lord. "I shall conclude with a colloquy reflecting on the divine mercy, thanking God our Lord who preserved me in life up to now; and resolving with his grace to amend my life for the future" (#61).

Thus, through the perception of myself and of my own poverty, weakness, and fragility I can come to grasp more perfectly the mystery of God, the mystery of the cross, the mystery of Christ who in his mercy compensates for, fills, overcomes and wipes out every fracture and inadequacy in my life. It is precisely to this level of a colloquy that Ignatius wishes to lead the exercitant. He does not want to arouse a sense of bitter guilt or a frigid and pessimistic realization of our situation. He wants to inspire us with admiration for the infinite, unspeakable mystery of mercy in which our lives . . . are inserted; for this mystery of grace which has followed us inexorably, penetrating us even to our most hidden, most negative and most unresponsive depths.

Bible readings

There are many biblical passages which we can use. In the psalms, especially the so-called penitential psalms (31, 37, 50, 101, 129, 142) the Bible makes its own the sentiments laid bare in the wealth and the exuberance of the psalmist's meditations. Thus all the psalms of repentance, of sorrow and of affliction can be used and will arouse our contrition, while at the same time praising the divine mercy.

I suggest especially psalm 50, the *Miserere,* with its confession of sin and hymn of praise. In it the psalmist expresses what Ignatius sought to tell us, perhaps better than he himself succeeded in doing.

Pastoral reflection

We often ask ourselves, and with a certain amount of anxiety, how we can provoke a due sense of sin and repentance. With this in view I suggest to you three brief pastoral reflections.

The first has to do with that sense of sin which is set before us and before the Christian people at least four times during the liturgy:

There is the penitential act at the beginning, which is a personal act ("*I* have sinned") and which centers on mercy (*Kyrie eleison* . . . Lord have mercy).

Next, I am touched by the sense of sin and of pardon which stands out especially at the moment of the eucharistic consecration: "My blood, which is being shed for the remission of sins." Here there is room for ample meditation on the sinfulness of humanity and on the superabundance of Christ's merciful blood, which is brought home to the consciences of the faithful through the deeply solemn words pronounced by the celebrant.

In the Our Father the entire community turns to the Father repeating the prayer of Jesus: "Forgive us our sins." This plea for pardon which is reiterated, is set before us as a fundamental Christian attitude, of us acknowledging ourselves as sinners.

Finally, at the moment of communion, we find the insistence on "Lamb of God who takes away the sins of the world." The Lamb of God in the holy eucharist is he who does away with the sins of the world, and the whole community invokes him and proclaims him.

If, then, the liturgy of the Mass inspires this rightful sense of sinfulness and of mercy, our pastoral action should certainly draw therefrom motives for educating the faithful.

The second reflection deals with the relationship between the sense of sin and the penitential celebrations, properly so called.

Unfortunately, all of us must recognize that in this connection we are not where we should be; and the 1983 Synod on the theme of reconciliation did not settle the problem concerning the crisis in personal reconciliation.

It is true that a good many still want personal reconciliation, when there are priests available. However, confession is in a state of crisis, and we need to face frankly the phenomenon of so many communions and so few confessions. We will need to seek for the profound causes of the situation and try to do away with them, beginning by reviving a deep personal sense of sin and of mercy, perhaps utilizing penitential practices closer to those of the ancient Church. I am thinking of something which would appeal to the essential dimension of the human conscience which is the sense of one's own frailty and proneness to sin, as confronted with the superabundant, unbelievable divine mercy (the two aspects are intimately connected). This sense of the superabundant divine mercy is rare, because we do not start from a realistic understanding of our own lack of correspondence. Further, we banalize human frailty by not acknowledging its character as an offence against God's mercy, its impenetrability toward the powerful action of the Spirit.

The third practical reflection has to do with our own confessions; they should in some manner reproduce the values mentioned above, in such a way as to nourish in ourselves the sense of sin and of mercy.

For this purpose, I would suggest that as a rule we begin our confession by praising and thanking God for his gifts, for his plans of love, for his goodness which expresses itself in the lives of each one of us, *confessio laudis*. In the light of God's gifts, my lack of correspondence with his designs can be expressed with more emphasis and with more personal truth.

Let us then ask through the intercession of the most Blessed Virgin Mary for this penitential spirit, which is so necessary in the moment of history we are living.

Guided By the Holy Spirit

(Homily for Tuesday of the Eighth Week of the Year)

The letter of Peter and the gospel of Mark

The First Letter of Peter, the beginning of which the liturgy had us read at Mass yesterday, goes on to speak of that "salvation of your souls" which is the end and purpose of our Christian endeavor. Let us listen once again to this passage assigned to this Tuesday of the eighth week of ordinary time:

"Concerning this salvation, prophets who prophesied about the grace that was to be yours, searched and investigated the time and circumstances that the Spirit of Christ within them indicated when it testified in advance to the sufferings destined for Christ and the glories to follow them. It was revealed to them that they were serving not themselves but you with regard to the things that have now been announced to you by those who preached the good news to you through the Holy Spirit sent from heaven, things into which angels longed to look. Therefore, gird up the loins of your mind, live soberly, and set your hopes completely on the grace to be brought to you at the revelation of Jesus Christ. Like obedient children do not act in compliance with the desires of your former ignorance but, as he who called you is holy, be holy yourselves in every aspect of your conduct, for it is written: 'Be holy, because I am holy' " (1 Pt 1:10-16).

This deep and meaningful text reaffirms the unity of the two alliances, the Old and the New Testaments, both of which are subjected to the Spirit of Christ. It was already the Spirit of Christ that the prophets were seeking to understand and it is in the Holy Spirit, sent down from heaven that the gospel is now being preached.

After the pneumatological presentation of salvation and of the unity of the two Testaments, Peter invites us to be on the watch. His words, "gird up the loins of your minds" correspond with the expression of the original Greek text. . . . We immediately think of Jesus' exhortation: "Be ready, with your loins girt, and lamps burning in your hands" (Lk 12:35).

Hence the pastoral consequences of the trinitarian proclamation of salvation is vigilance, and included in it, purification: "Do not act in compliance with the desires of your former ignorance." Don't let yourselves be shaped by a worldly mentality, but become holy. Model yourselves on the image of him who has called you.

The gospel reading is also related directly to yesterday's eucharistic liturgy. Jesus declared that it was impossible for the rich to enter the kingdom; but he added that with God all things are possible; and Peter realizes that in fact this miracle has taken place.

"Peter began to say to him: 'We have given up everything and followed you.' Jesus said: 'Amen, I say to you, there is no one who has given up home, or brothers or sisters, or mother or father, or children or lands for my sake and for the sake of the gospel who will not receive a hundred times more now in this present age: houses, and brothers and sisters, and mothers and children and lands, with persecutions, and eternal life in the age to come' " (Mk 10:28-31).

Two starting points for meditation

I suggest a few ideas for your meditative reflections on these two readings.

Peter's letter stresses the role, or better, the function of the prophets guided by the Spirit and of the gospel preachers acting in the times of the Spirit. The role of the prophets is to investigate and to scrutinize the importance and details of the manifestation of the paschal mystery; that of the gospel preachers is to proclaim such mysteries in the same Holy Spirit who permits us to investigate and to scrutinize the importance and details.

Lord, you call us to this task of investigating the times and circumstances of the manifestation of your mystery, amid today's confusion. Grant us, then, the grace to let ourselves be guided and led by your Spirit, that we may fulfill our prophetic mission in our day. Let us allow ourselves to be moved by the Holy Spirit so that we may proclaim the paschal mystery in the darkness and the anguish-ridden days we must go through.

Mark's passage helps us remember the explanation Ignatius gave in the colloquy after the first meditation on the three sins: "What have I done for Jesus Christ? What am I doing, and what should I do for him?" (#53). In fact, Peter can say in response to Jesus' words: "We have left all, and have followed you."

And we too can declare, with gratitude:

Lord, we have left all things for you, our life is dedicated to your cause, to the cause of the gospel. Give us the grace to open our eyes, to relish and enjoy the hundredfold with which even now you fill our lives while we look forward to the next life which you place in our hands in this eucharist.

The Repetitions and Additions
(#s 62-90)

The meditations for the First Week of the Exercises are, on the whole, wearisome and dry; they smack of the harshness of the path of purification, and our hardened hearts resist. But all this is a prelude to the glory of following Christ and a preparation for our paschal meeting with him.

We wish, then, to make a last effort to reflect on the first page of the First Week, or perhaps I should say, on the first day, because strangely enough Ignatius presents the five meditations in a single day, supposing that they are taken up again, repeated, and more deeply considered as necessary during the next six days.

We shall dwell on #s 62-72, and afterwards we shall briefly consider the Additions, #s 73-90, thus completing the readings of the text of the First Week. I shall not offer you an analysis but a simple commentary on the different paragraphs.

The importance of repetition

"The third exercise is a repetition of the first and the second, with three colloquies. After the preparatory prayer and the two preludes, I shall repeat the first and the second exercises with great attention, dwelling on those points in which I felt the most consolation or desolation, or greater spiritual sentiments. Afterwards, I shall use three colloquies" (#62).

It is good to emphasize at this point the importance of repetition that we find throughout Ignatius' work. The third and fourth meditations are a repetition of the first and second. The fifth is also a repetition of the previous ones but uses a more affective language.

I find especially interesting the following aspect of the method: Ignatius wants us to really absorb the material, not just to listen, learn, and grasp the logical meaning of what he says; he wants us to feel and taste it interiorly. Already in Annotation #2, he had said: "What satisfies and satiates the soul is not merely knowing a lot about the topic but feeling and tasting it interiorly." Faithful to this principle he wants us to go over the meditations themselves again, feeling them and tasting them affectively. In this way the road to a personalized faith begins, that is not just a learning of catechism. As regards this fundamental point of Christian pedagogy, we often fall short; we strive to help the faithful grow by doing the work for them. Still, there is no personalization of the faith without personal penetration. In the same Annotation #2, Ignatius warns those who propose a method for meditating or contemplating that they must explain "the subject of the meditation or contemplation faithfully, limiting themselves to touching the various points with a short and simple explanation." This way, those who contemplate may seize the nucleus of the mystery they contemplate, and then "by reflecting and reasoning they themselves may discover some aspect of it that will make them grasp it or apprehend it a little better, either through their own reasoning or by divine illumination." Hence, he is presupposing a personal activity based on one's own reasoning (even if not very profound) and on God's illumination, because it is the Lord who guides, accompanies and effects the understanding of such mystery.

He continues: "In this way [exercitants] will discover

more truths and more spiritual fruit than they would have if the giver of the Exercises had explained and developed more amply the sense of the mystery" (#2).

Obviously, there are times when it will be necessary to expand and to explain; however, if those to whom we offer our preaching and our catechism teaching do not contribute a certain amount of personal endeavor, our words will remain on the surface and in time will be forgotten.

That is why we set up in my diocese a "School of the Word." I always encourage the clergy who conduct it not to merely give a catechism lesson or a sermon, but to put the young people, and the public in general, in a position to appreciate the text of holy scripture thanks to their personal activity; to experience the joy of discovering the mystery which not only warms their hearts but urges them to act as well.

How repetition works

How does this penetration come about? By "dwelling on those points in which I felt the most consolations or desolations, or greater spiritual sentiments." We need to tend toward affectivity in order to leave aside whatever has not inspired us with either joy or fear, or at least some form of spiritual sentiment. Thus meditation becomes an instrument of purification and liberation for the heart. It purifies our affectivity in the crucible of our sentiments; it liberates the heart from what is negative and shapes it.

Once again we are facing an important aspect of Christian pedagogy. Unfortunately, the mediocre Christian has no deep interior affections and shows a slight amount of emotion only when joining in on the singing of a familiar hymn in church.

Still, no one comes to a personal, convinced, witness-bear-ing faith without an experience of a strong impulse of interior affectivity. Without this, religious practice is merely a question of habit or a purely cerebral experience, quickly exhausted.

And I never tire of commending the exercise of the *lectio divina* in times like ours, because it stirs up affectivity when we are in front of the reality of the mystery.

In the past, when faith and culture were homogeneous, interior affectivity could be suscitated by community functions.

Today, on the other hand, in our confused, unravelling, fragmented society, unless faith has this personal dimension, it cannot survive long. Without the personal welcoming of the Spirit, Christianity remains a superficial patina, easily worn off in a foreign, alienated, diverse and worldly environment.

This Ignatian method of repetition is very helpful, therefore, and so is the *lectio divina;* for it fills the heart either with consolation or desolation (in the course of which we must overcome the enemy, and hence our personal activity is stimulated once again).

I think that for people like us, who make the Exercises every year, it is possible to call to mind moments in past Exercises in which we have felt consolation, repugnance and struggles more keenly and to re-live them now by interiorly going through them again. Hence, the more we journey forward, the more we enrich ourselves by this spiritual and emotive memory, which makes the life of faith more profound, more intense, more closely linked to our personal dynamism.

The fruit (#63)

In #63 we receive the fruit of the repetition proposed in #62. This is presented in the form of a prayer, that pleas for three graces in a triple colloquy: with our Lady, with the Son, and with the Father.

This formula of the triple request, which is found several times in the Exercises, is an intense supplication for highly important graces, and it shows the order in which we should ask for them: through Mary, from Jesus, and from the Father. Mary is the one to whom we have recourse in the crucial moments of our spiritual Christian journey.

"The first colloquy is with our Lady, so that she may obtain for me from her Son three graces: the first that I may acquire an intimate knowledge and detestation of my sins; the second, that I may realize the disorder in my actions and, detesting them, bring order into my life; the third, that I may come to know the world and thus, detesting it, may keep myself far from earthly vanities. The second colloquy, in the same manner: with the Son so that he may obtain these graces from the Father. . . . The third colloquy in the same manner with the Father, so that he, the eternal Lord, may grant them to me."

These three graces include the labor of purification which accompanies all Christian life, and in which we can, therefore, see ourselves reflected as we meditate on them at length. I have not found in the First Week a meditation richer than these few lines.

The first grace is to receive from God through the inpouring of the Spirit an intimate knowledge of my sins and to detest them. This means interiorizing the grace of penance, and it is the mature fruit of that grace. This is the interior attitude of repugnance at the offence against God, not only for my past sins, but also for future ones. This attitude should act as an interior defence even in the moments of my greatest weakness, because henceforth it has taken root in my own conscience.

We need to educate our Christian people through a

heightened spiritual affectivity to this instinctive disgust for sin, to this instinctive love for divine order, the divine plan of our salvation. We need to make them want to be true sons and daughters, and not to break this bond for any reason. The cardinal point of Christian conversion, the goal of moral education, is not merely to impart the knowledge of good and evil, but the instinctive repugnance for evil, and the instinctive inclination toward the good, which is salvation in Christ.

The second grace: to "realize the disorder in my actions and, detesting them, bring order into my life."

The mention of the words "order" and "disorder" reminds us of the First Principle and Foundation. "Order" here means the order of creation, of redemption, of grace; it is the trinitarian order in which we are called to give praise to God. And interior knowledge, which can be strongly affected by disorder, is a gift which makes us perceive which of our daily actions are not ways to assimilate us to Jesus. It helps us to know which ones run counter to the logic and the order of the gospel and are not fully in line with the end for which we are created, or at least not to the degree and in the manner required by God's plan.

Let us then ask for the grace of discovering such disorder; and this discovery will surprise us. We shall realize how many of our actions are not consonant with the filial attitude that should be ours, but rather leave it out of consideration. At the same time, however, it delivers us, it unbinds us interiorly, by showing us the truth about ourselves. We asked, at the start of the Exercises, for adaptability and joy in the mystery; the first deliverance is this one of purification, when we recognize disorder in ourselves and hence feel poor before God and the perfection of the kingdom.

The discovery of disorder in oneself is that which the saints made when they recognized how far they were from the demands of the living and transfiguring mystery of the kingdom. This discovery inspires us to battle, directs us to the gospel order of life, makes people healthily restless, that is, attentive in living the beatitudes and responding to the powerful action of the purifying Spirit. Disorder is in fact resistance to the Spirit who wants to see us saints in the Son.

Is it possible to find in Ignatius' *Autobiography* some passages that could serve as examples to this?

One interesting section is #35, where he describes the beginning of his trip to Jerusalem. Early in 1523, two years after his conversion, Ignatius is waiting to board a ship in Barcelona where a problem presents itself: What does it mean, to travel according to the gospel spirit? "Certain friends offered to accompany him, but he preferred to leave alone; his unique desire was to have God alone as his refuge. One day some persons urged him to take along a certain companion since he was ignorant of both Italian and Latin. They praised this person to the skies and said that he would be of much help to him. He answered that even if this person was the son or the brother of the duke of Cardona, he would not accept him as his companion. He intended to practice three virtues: charity, faith and hope. Taking along a companion, he would have expected help and assistance from *him*, had he gotten hungry or into any kind of trouble. Thus, he would have to place his trust in this person and would have come to love him on account of all those favors." In those days Ignatius took the gospel literally and felt that if he allowed himself to have a companion he would have violated his trust in God alone. "He, instead, wished to place his trust and his affection and his hope in God alone. This is what he said, and this is what he felt deep in his heart." This is a grace of intimate awareness of a possible disorder, so as to avoid and abhor it.

Next came the problem of provisions for the journey: "He

would have wanted to embark not only without any companions but also without any provisions. When the embarkation proceedings began he obtained from the shipmaster free passage since he had no money, but on condition that he should bring along his own provisions." The problem seemed insoluble. Ignatius did not want to take along any provisions, but to board the ship he had to have some.

"When he went to buy bread new perplexities assailed him: 'Is this the hope and faith that you placed in God and which you never wanted to abandon?' and so on. This doubt was so perplexing that he was much tormented" (#36). There you have the sense of gospel order; what must I do to conform myself fully to Jesus?

"He did not know what to do; on both sides of the question he found valid arguments. He decided, therefore, to consult his confessor. He told the latter of his eager desire to seek perfection and to choose what could give the greatest glory to God." His confessor told him to take with him whatever he might manage to gather, and so he felt reassured and went out to beg. "But on the deck of the ship he noticed that he still had five or six small coins which he had received when he went begging from door to door. He left them on a table which he found on the dock." Having already bought the necessary provisions, he had begun to fear that those few coins might create in him a sense of security not conformable to the gospel.

It seems to me that this text gives us the idea of what Ignatius intended by this second grace: to "realize the disorder in my actions and, detesting them, bring order into my life."

The third grace: "That I may come to know the world and thus, detesting it, may keep myself far from all earthly vanities."

Here we have another very important grace, especially for

one who has responsibilities in the Church. Ignatius had experienced worldly vanities; he had desired and sought them. Hence, he knew how vanity and ambition find their way into the court and the ecclesiastical spheres, into kings' palaces, bishops' dwellings and canonical stalls. He knew well of ambitions and vanities regarding one's manner of dressing, of administering one's apartment, one's car, one's bank account and even one's culture. Everything can be spoiled by vanity. We see how even the most insignificant titles, the strangest honorary decorations are sought after because vanity, like the air, penetrates everywhere.

Ignatius knows that this worldliness casts a shadow over the truth of the gospel; it is an insidious fog, a smog which attacks the stones of cathedrals, devouring them from within.

This is why he insistently makes us ask for disgust of earthly vanities, for the capacity of considering them with irony, with detachment and also with alarm, because it is certainly true that sometimes even the cedars of Lebanon fall before ambition and prestige. There are persons who perhaps have served God with dedication and generosity, yet still get their backs up for a point of honor, of vanity, and lose that flexibility which they had acquired through patient and humble service.

It is, then, very useful to repeat the triple colloquy of #63 to obtain these three graces which we do not possess and which are given to us by the Spirit, not through simple conviction of the mind, but through a transformation of our affections. We ask these insistently of Mary, the mother of love, truth, humility, evangelical simplicity; and then of Jesus Christ so that he may obtain them for us from the Father. We can use this moving prayer: "Soul of Christ, sanctify me; body of Christ, save me; blood of Christ, inebriate me; water from Christ's side, wash me." Finally we turn to the Father, concluding by the prayer taught us by Jesus.

For Ignatius, in fact, every meditation of the Exercises should end with the Our Father, with that cry of sonship, of trust and abandonment.

Meditation on hell (#s 65-71)

Omitting the fourth exercise (#64) which is a repetition of the third, I go on to the fifth (#65), which reads as follows: "Meditation on hell; after a preparatory prayer and two preludes, it includes five points and a colloquy."

The five points, familiar to all, call for an application of the five senses (sight, hearing, taste, smell and touch) to the pains of hell, and thus even uncultured people can be introduced to the mystery of iniquity, to the understanding of how infinite mercy, when rejected, is changed into human damnation. We cannot omit this meditation, even if we have to give it in a more modernized form, because it shows us the true outcome of a refusal to let oneself be loved by God and transformed into the Son. It represents the foiling of the work of creation and redemption: the disorder which, taking root in the human heart, torments it from within. Even though this meditation may appear harsh, it is a very accurate theological meditation, showing starkly how the destruction of the divine plan leads to the damnation of the soul, not to its salvation. Persons who have despised the substantive reference points of their lives, refusing the trustful love for God the Father, respect for their neighbors and for the harmony of creation, remain cut off from any possibility of achieving their purpose as human beings. God loves them and continues to love them in his mercy; but they reject that love because of their own misfortune, just as they reject all bonds between themselves, other persons and even things. Unfortunately infernal situations do arise even in this life, when persons close themselves off from God and from their

neighbors, hating everyone and everything, even themselves. The moral degradation brought on by drugs leads to
this total refusal of any relationship and to this terrible
unhappiness. The victim needs continual stimulation to
have a minimum reason for surviving. Yet even these "hells"
within a person's heart are still and always subject to the
divine mercy and hence are capable of opening up again to
embrace and to welcome.

I think that today we should use the meditation on hell,
insisting less on the visual and cosmological elements, and
more on the anthropological ones: anguish, solitude, frustration, despair. These are sentiments which everyone knows,
and which are contrary to God's plan for humanity, namely
happiness, fullness, order, peace and harmony.

The utility of the Additions (#s 73-90)

Having offered some suggestions for #s 65-71, I invite you
to reread calmly the Additions which conclude the First
Week (#s 73-90).

Why did Ignatius use these additional notes? The reason
is very simple: "to make the Exercises better and to find more
easily what is desired" (#73).

It is assumed, therefore, that the exercise of prayer is
dependent on slight but important pedagogical, psychological and spiritual conditions. Some of these Additions are also
useful in the liturgy, in children's, youths' and family prayers.
Neglecting the psychological and spiritual factors leads to
failure; it is like wanting to fly without wings. And yet, often
enough, we are negligent on these points, and we do not
teach them to others. Is it any wonder the faithful say that
they do not know how to pray, to recollect themselves?

True, prayer is a mysterious gift of God, a most precious
one, enabling us to open ourselves to God. However, this
opening of self calls for a minimum of conditions in one's

physical, psychological and somatic surroundings, without which one prays in a superficial, distracted, tiresome and burdensome manner. Then Mass is wearisome, sermons are a bother, and so are catechism lessons and the rosary, because whenever one does not enter wholeheartedly into a practice, it remains external and only irritates without nourishing. If we do not teach the faithful how to reach at least a minimum of mental discipline, our Christianity will always be rather superficial, and both children and young people will soon forget the elements of the catechism we have stuffed their heads with. If, on the contrary, we observe certain conditions, the children, young people and even adults will be able to enjoy prayer and silence; and they will discover within themselves that mystery which we had been wearing ourselves out trying to explain to them from the outside.

The ten Additions for a proper discipline of the mind are therefore highly useful; and we must consider them, not perhaps so much to the letter, but in their Spirit, so that in fact we can give similar advice to others.

I remember one such which has remained deeply fixed in my mind after many years. It is found in the third and fourth Additions (#s 75-76). After ordination to the priesthood the Jesuits go through a third year of novitiate and make the Exercises over again. I did this in Austria, and the instructor for the month, a German priest, began each of the five daily meditations with this very brief suggestion: *Sich ruhig vor Gott werden lassen*—Let your soul grow calm before God. This is an essential requisite. When there is a cry from the heart, a profound interior emotion, it is possible to enter upon prayer immediately. However, as a rule, it is most difficult to go from one's daily occupations and distractions to a state of prayer without first calming oneself down, without recollecting oneself, without being quiet for a few minutes, and then acknowledging that one is unworthy to speak to God, to adore him, and finally humbling oneself before him. Then prayer loosens up, and the person who thought he or she was dry, sad, with no interest in anything, finds himself or herself again in the right frame of mind for praying. If we teach our people this discipline we shall in general find them very grateful.

Conclusion: God is not afraid of sin

After having explained the meaning of the final paragraphs of the First Week, I should like to give you a few words of F. Rossi de Gasperis, S.J., in one of his comments on the First Week of the Exercises: "In God's creative act (understanding this to be a global, creative and redemptive act, in which God gives himself entirely to humanity in Christ) there is room for all the sins of the world, because God knows how to come back home." I was taken by this expression because it explains very well and in capsule form what sin is in God's plan. God is not afraid of sin, nor is there a single one, however serious it may be, that God can't deal with, or at which he remains surprised. True, holy scripture affirms that in God we can find anger, indignation, wrath, and paternal threats for sin. But these sentiments, applied to God, are a form of his almighty, burning mercy. God always knows how to come back home, because Jesus is the man who brings everything back with himself in superabundance.

The contemplation of sin places us, then, before the most horrid sins, but we see them in the light of God who is afraid of nothing, who knows how to take everything back in hand and to reconvert it into grace, how to overturn evil and draw good from it.

These are the truths which the First Week wants to bring us to realize, inviting us to meditation on divine mercy and on our sins.

In Secret Before God

(Homily for Ash Wednesday)

Penance in the heart

The liturgy of Ash Wednesday proposes to us a passage taken from the book of Joel, in which the prophet exhorts us to do penance:

"Yet even now, says the Lord, return to me with your whole heart, with fasting and weeping and mourning. Rend your hearts, not your garments and return to the Lord your God; for gracious and merciful is he, slow to anger, rich in kindness and relenting in punishment. Perhaps he will again relent and leave behind him a blessing. Offerings and libations for the Lord your God. Blow the trumpet in Zion; proclaim a fast, call an assembly. Gather the people, notify the congregation, assemble the elders, gather the children and the infants at the breast. Let the bridegroom quit his room, and the bride her chamber; between the porch and the altar let the priests, the ministers of the Lord, speak and say: 'Spare O Lord, your people, and make not your heritage a reproach, with the nations ruling over them. Why should they say among the peoples "where is their God?" ' " (Jl 2:12-18).

Joel is best known as the prophet of the Holy Spirit, of Pentecost, so much so that Peter, starting his first sermon to the crowd gathered in Jerusalem, quoted some verses from his writings.

In the text read today, however, the prophet urges the

people to be converted, to do penance. This message was inspired by an external happening—the plague of grasshoppers which was devastating Judea. The Lord alone can rescue the people from this scourge, and hence it is necessary to implore him with prayers and fasting while detesting one's sins. For us, it is useful to listen to this insistence on inner penance: "Return to me with your whole heart. . . . Rend your hearts, not your garments."

Penance is something that must be lived interiorly, in the intimate movements of spiritual affection, as Ignatius teaches us in the meditations on sin. He wants us to experience it in the form of tears and sentiments of compunction, which determine a person's actions and exterior choices.

Only the interior life is acceptable to the "Lord our God, merciful and kind, slow to anger and rich in mercy, who is saddened over our misfortunes," because this is the attitude by which a person recognizes that God is tender and merciful of heart, and hence the person seeks to be in prayerful resonance with the heart of Christ.

Before God

The gospel passage from Matthew also insists on the interior aspect of penance: "Take care not to perform righteous deeds in order that people may see them; otherwise you will have no recompense from your heavenly Father. When you give alms, do not blow a trumpet before you, as the hypocrites do in the synagogues and in the streets, to win the praise of others. Amen, I say to you, they have received their reward. But when you give alms, do not let your left hand know what your right is doing, so that your almsgiving may be secret, and your Father who sees in secret will repay you. When you pray, do not be like the hypocrites, who love to stand and pray in the synagogues and on street corners so that others may see them. Amen, I say to you, they have received their reward. But when you pray, go to your inner room, close the door, and pray to your Father in secret. And your Father who sees in secret will repay you. . . . When you fast, do not look gloomy, like the hypocrites. They neglect their appearance so that they may appear to others to be fasting. Amen, I say to you, they have received their reward. But when you fast, anoint your head and wash your face, so that you may not appear to be fasting, except to your Father who is hidden; and your Father, who sees what is hidden will repay you" (Mt 6:1-6.16-18).

Notice the triple repetition of "doing in secret," "in the sight of your Father who sees in secret" and the way this is contrasted with "before others," "to win the praise of others," "to be seen by them." Here another characteristic of the Christian way is brought out: the way of liberty. This liberty pays attention to God alone, and hence takes no account of eventual, possibly justified, recognition, approbation and rewards. For these too we should thank the Lord; and yet, what is solely important, definitive, and absolutely sufficient, is God's approval, his reward in secret. Let your almsgiving remain secret; let your prayer remain secret; let your fasting remain secret. These are words on which I reflect frequently because a bishop is fortunate enough to be able to perform in secret a great many actions of forgiveness; he can indeed experience in secret many humiliations, many renunciations, make important choices which will never be known by the public, which will never be sanctioned or earn him merit. Even historical research will never be able to ascertain the motives of a bishop's secret actions.

Think, for instance, of Charles Borromeo or Cardinal Ferrari. Many facts of their lives have been brought to light through letters and historical documents but most of their deeds were performed in secret, and only God knew of them, recognized them, and rewarded them. All this corresponds with the absolute ethical character of a person's choices and hence with the absolute quality and service of our one Lord, which is proper of the choices made by a bishop.

When I happen to hear judgments on my confreres in the episcopate, on their manner of running their dioceses, I keep thinking that even the most accurate judgments never reach the marrow of a person's pastoral action, never really tell what a person has or has not done, because these are external judgments made up of human opinions and evaluations. Meanwhile, the ultimate reason for certain decisions, the deep motivation that underlies the making of certain decisions, occur in secret, before God. A decision that seeks to be faithful to Christ, both in conscience and in light of the many evangelical choices, in the end does not have to be defended in front of any person.

Such is the case with all the great ethical choices that concern particular Church situations, groups of people and collectivities, which certainly would gain by being approved and confirmed by public opinion, but which, particularly in their most delicate and decisive phases, must be lived in the secret of the Father. And the Father who sees all and knows when a decision might not have been entirely pure or evangelical will correct and purify it. Matthew's passage strengthens us when we seek in penance what is interior, what reaches the heart, especially what places us in the right attitude toward the Father, by whom we know we are loved, understood, upheld, rewarded, corrected if necessary, but always with infinite mercy.

The King's Summons (#s 91-98)

The call of the earthly king

The Second Week of Ignatius' Exercises begins with an activity whose title describes only the purpose, not the literary type, of the writing.

"The call of the earthly king helps us to contemplate the life of the eternal king" (#91). We are invited to contemplate the life of the eternal king; and all the following meditations will be drawn from the gospels.

Even though this preliminary exercise is not really a meditation or a contemplation, it follows the usual development. First of all we shall read #91 in its context; then we shall seek to consider more specifically the meaning and the dynamics of the exercise proposed to us. In the third place I shall suggest a Bible reading and consider more particularly the final colloquy; finally we shall reflect on the message contained in this text as we find it expressed in the *Autobiography*.

Examination of #s 91-98 in the context of the Exercises

After mentioning the title, #91 continues as follows:

"The usual preparatory prayer. Then the first prelude, which is a mental representation of the place. Here we try to imagine the synagogues, the towns and country where

Jesus Christ our Lord preached." Here we can already see the desire of fellowship. We wish to follow Jesus and be inspired by his life. (I recently was able to revisit this locale, because I spent a few days of prayer in Galilee, experiencing all the charm of Jesus' land—its hills and its lake. It was easy for me to imagine the synagogue of Capharnaum, whose remains have recently been unearthed, the towns of Corosaim and of Bethsaida, of Cana and of Nazareth as they were in the days when Jesus preached in Galilee.)

"The second prelude consists in asking for the grace I desire: namely, begging our Lord for the grace of not showing myself deaf to his call but rather ready and eager to fulfill his most holy will." We are, then, faced with a call; while we are seeking to organize our lives in a manner conformable with God's will, we find the will of Jesus, which is already calling us.

This exercise (#s 92-97) has two distinct parts each with three points:

In #92 we are given the parable, the image of the earthly king, "appointed directly by God our Lord, to whom all princes and all Christians owe respect and obedience."

In #93 we see proclaimed the call of this king, who is engaged in a great undertaking: "to win back all the territories of the infidels." He invites us to follow him in this. But whoever wishes to follow him must share, in equal measure, in his sufferings, labors and successes.

In #94 we are invited to reflect on what sort of response his subjects should give to so generous and humane a king. Whoever would not accept the proposal of such a king should be despised by all and considered a wretch (the Spanish word is "unworthy knight"). This is a key word.

The second part of the exercise is the application of the parable to Jesus Christ.

"First Point: if the call of an earthly king to his subjects deserves attention, how much more worthy of consideration is it to see our Lord, the eternal king, who has summoned all humankind before him, and who calls each single one, saying: 'It is my will to subject to my sway all the world and all my adversaries and thus enter into the glory of my Father. For this reason those who wish to come with me must labor with me, so that after following me in my sufferings they may also follow me in glory' " (#95).

"Second Point: I think that all reasonable persons with good sense, will offer themselves without any reservations to this undertaking" (#96).

Then we find a new element, not present in the parable. The call goes out to all who wish "to engage themselves more fully and to distinguish themselves in the service of their eternal king and universal Lord," who propose to make "an offering of greater value and greater importance" (#97), saying: "Eternal Lord of the universe, with your favor and your help I make my offering before your infinite goodness and before your glorious mother and all the saints of the heavenly court. I want and desire, and it is my firm decision, provided it is for your greater service and praise, to imitate you in enduring injury, scorn and all poverty, whether material or spiritual, if your most holy Majesty wishes to choose me and to receive me in this kind of life" (#98).

This, therefore, is the basic exercise, preceding all contemplations on the life of Jesus, and it must be repeated twice a day (#99). It is not too clear just what Ignatius intended by this; perhaps he wants the exercitant to repeat it various times for several days, until he has penetrated into the meaning of this key reading.

The meaning and dynamism of the parable of the king

Wishing to penetrate at least a little more into this key reading, let us begin by asking ourselves: Why is so much attention given to an exercise of this kind?

The answer is simple: Because it is, so to speak, the Principle and Foundation of the rest of the Exercises.

It is a second Principle and Foundation, and as such is not a part of the Second Week. In fact, the meditation which follows this one (on the incarnation) is entitled: "First day; first contemplation" (#101).

This exercise is the key to understanding the life of Jesus, to understanding the gospels which, as he mentions in #100, should be put into the hands of the exercitant at this point in the Exercises. He or she may meditate on them along with the *Imitation of Christ* and the lives of the saints: the *Imitation*, so that we may emulate Jesus, not so much by learning the gospels by heart but by adopting his attitudes and lifestyle; the lives of the saints because they have put the gospel into practice.

This meditation on the gospel texts (which is proposed for the rest of the Exercises) is not intended to lead to an exegetical expertise; its purpose is to make us aware of the Spirit which inspired Jesus, to assimilate it and put it into practice right away through resolutions and decisions taken during the Exercises.

Precisely for this reason we shall question ourselves more specifically on the text, desiring to understand its meaning and its dynamism.

We have already mentioned that this is a parable, similar for example to the one Nathan related to King David.

"The Lord sent Nathan to David and when he came to him he said: 'Judge this case for me. In a certain town there were two men, one rich, the other poor. The rich man had flocks and herds in great number, but the poor man had nothing at all, except one little ewe lamb that he had bought. He nourished her, and she grew up with him and his children; she shared the food he had, and drank from his cup, and slept in his bosom. She was like a daughter to him. Now the rich man received a visitor, but he would not take from his own flocks and herds to prepare a meal for the wayfarer who had come to him; instead he took the poor man's ewe lamb and made a meal of it for his visitor' " (2 Sam 12:1-4).

Nathan related this parable to awaken the king's sense of justice, to test him regarding his duty of defending the rights of the poor, which was so keen in David. Then, a fortiori he challenged him: "You did worse things yourself!" The dynamism of the call of the earthly king is the same, but the conclusion is to the contrary. Ignatius appeals to the sentiments of the exercitant, which he assumes are noble, not mediocre. Knightly sentiments proper to the feudal world where loyalty of vassal toward his lord counted very much; when he had been given a feud he had to show himself faithful and grateful to the one who had displayed trust in him. Sentiments proper to a monarchical world, where the reference is to the figure of an unquestioned leader, and proper also to a world where sacred duties are supreme, especially when this leader is approved by God and sets about a great religious undertaking, for instance a crusade.

Ignatius reasons that whoever is moved by noble sentiments toward his earthly king will be moved even more profoundly toward Jesus, the universal king and Lord. He is appealing, then, to that which is most personal in his contemporaries: sincerity, nobility, loyalty. If Jesus is truly the Lord, then without doubt he deserves much more than I could give him, even though I would consider it an extraordinary stroke of good fortune to be called by an earthly king.

Through the parable exercitants understand the greatness, the risk and the beauty of the undertaking proposed by Jesus. They feel an urge to offer themselves, to make a more total oblation than they would make to a monarch or any human leader.

From the description of this dynamism we realize that today, unfortunately, it is very difficult to imagine a situation in which loyalty and gratitude of this feudal kind would come into play, like knightly courage, fidelity to a monarch, or reverence as regards an undertaking approved by God. Today we do not find ourselves in similar situations, because we live in days of uncertainty. Various ideologies have attempted to evoke similar sentiments and perhaps the latest to date is Marxism; those who believed in it felt a deep attachment to an enterprise which they considered great, to unquestioned chieftains, almost mythical figures, who had arisen from the people and had acquired a charismatic power. But since the decay of Marxism, such reputations have come to be seen as false.

I have heard many, many attempts at re-writing the parable, substituting new terms for its old ones but they have never convinced me.

We are in a situation resembling that of the New Testament, in which people lacked real reference points because the civil authority in those days was pagan. I think, therefore, that it is preferable to skip the first part of the exercise, and to place ourselves right away in the presence of Jesus, the only Son of the Father, the firstborn of all creation, the firstborn from the dead, the definitive Messiah, the Savior, the center of history, who has given himself up for me. Jesus, to whom it is right to say: "In you we trust, O Lord; you laid down your life for us, and we offer it back to you; we want to follow you because we owe you everything."

While the world at the end of the Middle Ages still had secular references which were of help to it, we must renew the direct contact with the figure of Jesus in the gospel.

A biblical reading: the call of Peter

I am suggesting to you, therefore, a Bible reading. There are many pages of the gospels which can be meditated on to help us understand what Ignatius wished to teach us by his parable, and which express the heart of the New Testament and of the Christian undertaking: to follow Jesus, to be with him, to share in his tasks, to be a disciple. Texts which speak of the call are many.

However, the passage in Luke 5:1-11 seems particularly significant to me. In Peter we can grasp what it means to get enthusiastic over Jesus, and to decide to follow him.

"When the crowd was pressing in on Jesus and listening to the word of God, he was standing by the lake of Gennesaret. He saw two boats there alongside the lake; the fishermen had disembarked and were washing their nets. Getting into one of the boats, the one belonging to Simon, he asked him to put out a short distance from the shore. Then he sat down and taught the crowds from the boat. After he had finished speaking he said to Simon: 'Put out into the deep water, and lower your nets for a catch.' Simon said in reply: 'Master, we have worked hard all night and have caught nothing, but at your command I will lower the nets.' When they had done this they caught a great number of fish, and their nets were tearing. They signalled to their partners in the other boat to come to help them. They came and filled both boats so that they were in danger of sinking. When Simon Peter saw this, he fell at the knees of Jesus and said: 'Depart from me, Lord, for I am a sinful man.' For astonishment at the catch of fish they had made seized him and all those with him, and likewise James and John, the sons of Zebedee, who were partners of Simon. Jesus said to Simon, 'Do not be afraid; from now on you will be catching men.' When they brought their boats to the shore they left everything and followed him."

What sentiments does Peter experience?

First of all he feels very gratified over the trust shown him by Jesus, who selected his boat to preach from; he feels himself the object of the benevolent trust of this Rabbi, who already held the crowd spellbound, and who is paying attention to him now.

Furthermore, he feels himself repaid a hundredfold for the little confidence he did show when he cast his nets into the sea again. The huge catch, in fact, puts Peter in the forefront of all his fellow fishermen.

At this point, Peter realizes who he is, and his unworthiness as regards what he can now grasp as a divine mystery. In fact, while in verse 5 he used the term "Master," in verse 8 he now addresses Jesus as "Lord."

Finally, conscious of his unworthiness in the presence of this mystery, he feels once again overwhelmed beyond all expectation by Jesus' trust, and by being called to collaborate in a much more important undertaking than he could have ever imagined; an undertaking capable of arousing his messianic enthusiasm.

In Peter thus depicted we can see portrayed our own condition as redeemed Christians, pardoned, made worthy of Christ's confidence, and called by him, invited to come after him on the road of fellowship and evangelical salvation.

The colloquy (#98): the Jesus whom we are following

Let us now take up again the final colloquy of the exercise, found in #98, which we have already considered, because what emerges especially here is the meaning of the key given to us in the parable of the call of the king.

When the disciple—realizing that he or she is a pardoned and forgiven Christian, called personally by Jesus—resolves to adopt the gospel way of following, he or she needs to know the conditions for doing this. Today there are few who look these conditions squarely and clearly in the face. So many young people, though generous, are merely satisfied with a following that mainly inspires enthusiasm, with some inevitable sacrifices—but they go no farther.

Ignatius' merit in this exercise is to state explicitly and courageously the meaning of gospel following based on the beatitudes, and to spell out what it implies, making it a key for understanding the whole life of Christ.

Who is this Jesus whom you wish to follow? It is the Jesus who has nowhere to lay his head (the poor Jesus); it is the Jesus who will be rejected by the ancients, by the high priests and the scribes (Jesus insulted, despised and humiliated). Thus, we are called to follow Jesus, poor and humbled, whose whole life contradicts the ambitions, the vanities, the possessiveness proper to worldliness.

Ignatius clearly warns the exercitant: only following *this* Jesus will bring one to the freedom of heart, will overcome the conditioning wrought by the world, ever ready to attack the choices that lead to the kingdom. Without this kind of following we run the risk of deluding ourselves even in our choices for Jesus, the risk of choosing a self-gratifying line of action, one leading to success even if it involves some fatigue. What we seek here is an undertaking which will open our hearts to Jesus' choices as indicated in the beatitudes: Jesus who marches toward Jerusalem, toward the cross; the Jesus of the paschal mystery. We are called to study in the school of *this* Jesus, to share in his filial liberty, in his consciousness of being a Son, which he expressed historically in being poor, humiliated and rejected. We are called to recognize that in this way alone will Jesus guide us to filial liberty.

It is a lesson that we keep forgetting, day after day, and which our *lectio divina* will remind us of daily. For this reason the *lectio divina* has such a value for transforming us according to the gospel. But it needs to be read with a reading guide, the very one proposed by Jesus in the most important moments of his ministry, when he speaks of the rejected Messiah, the Messiah who must suffer. Jesus labors for weeks, months and years to make the apostles accept that *this* is the Messiah, the true Messiah; and the apostles in their turn struggle all the way to the resurrection to accept that *this* is the Messiah who guides us to life, that *this* is the path leading to the kingdom.

We might say that the key to understanding the reading proposed by Ignatius for the gospel meditation which will follow, is the same one that we find in the great synthetic passages of the New Testament, which serve as keys for all biblical history, in particular for those texts referring to Christ. Among these passages the most significant is, perhaps, that of the christological hymn in the letter to the Philippians: "Christ . . . who though he was in the form of God did not regard equality with God something to be grasped; rather he emptied himself, taking the form of a slave, coming in human likeness and found human in appearance; he humbled himself, becoming obedient to death, even death on a cross. Because of this, God greatly exalted him and bestowed on him the name that is above every name, that at the name of Jesus every knee should bend of those in heaven and on earth and under the earth, and every tongue confess that Jesus Christ is Lord to the glory of God the Father" (Phil 2:5-11).

This is what Ignatius has us ask for: Lord, we wish to follow you with your very own sentiments, you who did not consider your equality with God as a treasure to be jealously kept, but who stripped yourself of it and became a servant, like unto human beings, humiliating yourself, and making yourself obedient to the death of the cross.

Ignatius seeks to enter, through prayerful reading, into

these sentiments of Jesus, which are the key to the history of salvation, the way leading to true Christian liberty; they are the environment in which it is possible to make evangelical choices tending to the end for which we were created: to praise, to revere and to serve God by making ourselves like Christ and becoming sons and daughters with him and in him.

The question here is not about a certain joyful baptismal consciousness, but about entering upon the way of the beatitudes, about Jesus' entry into Jerusalem, about his passion, death and resurrection.

Ignatius' testimony in his Autobiography

In conclusion, we want to ask ourselves whether we find in the *Autobiography* this key to the Bible readings.

We observe at once that, starting with his conversion, this is the theme most often repeated in Ignatius' writings: to be like Jesus in his humiliations. It recurs with unforeseen and surprising variations.

Let us recall, for instance, what happened to him in Jerusalem. Eager to return to Mount Olivet to see once more the footprints left by Jesus on the stone from which he mounted to heaven, he dropped away from the group of pilgrims, and went back alone. "When the friars of the convent noted that he had gone off without any guide, they began to search for him anxiously. Thus, while he was coming down from the olive grove he met a Christian of the enclosure who worked for the convent and who, wielding a big stick and being furiously angry, seized him violently by one arm. The pilgrim allowed himself to be led away without offering any resistance, but the man continued to hold on to him. While going along one street, still held by the convent's servant, he received great consolations from the Lord; it seemed to him that he saw Christ continually above him. And this consolation lasted with great intensity until he reached the convent" (#48).

During one of his trips to Italy Ignatius was made a prisoner by some soldiers who stripped him, searched him, bound him and wanted to take him to their captain: "On the way, the pilgrim kept remembering how Christ had been bound and led away. . . . They traversed three crowded streets, but he went along without any sadness; instead, he was very glad and happy. As a rule he addressed people in a polite but informal way. He did this for a religious motive, convinced that Christ and the apostles spoke this way. While he was being hurried along the streets though, the idea came to him that on this occasion it might be well to give up his custom, and to address the captain with the words: 'Your Lordship.' Fear of possible torture also suggested this to him. But no sooner had he realized that this was a temptation, he said to himself, 'I will not call him "Lordship," nor will I make any reference to him, nor will I take off my biretta' " (#52).

His resolve to imitate Jesus is shown especially in the long ecclesiastical hearings which he had to undergo, and which he relates in detail, one by one. We know, in fact, that Ignatius suffered much from the ecclesiastical establishment, but in his descriptions of it we find only serenity and simplicity, not bitterness; he even notes the joy he experienced when he was accused unjustly.

From this attitude arose that liberty regarding the ecclesiastical establishment which brought him to Rome so that he might serve it close at hand, although he was not ignorant of its defects and limitations. The powerful desire to be like Jesus helped him to see with love even the delays and the ponderousness of the Church's action.

Among many similar episodes let me cite the one we read in #69. One day, there came to visit him in prison "Fr. Francesco de Mendoza (later Cardinal of Burgos) accompanied by Mr. Frias. They asked him familiarly how he felt about being in jail and whether being a prisoner was hard for him to bear. He told them: 'I will give you the same reply that this very day I gave to a lady who showed great compassion on seeing me in prison. I told her: By that you only show that you have no desire to be jailed for the love of God. Does prison seem such a terrible thing to you? As for me, I assure you, if I wore all the chains and bonds in Salamanca, I would desire even more for the love of God.' "

These passages from the *Autobiography* are enough to show us the importance of the exercise preliminary to the Second Week to help us enter into the sentiments of Jesus who became our Savior through his life of hiddenness and humility. This path, sought for and lovingly chosen, is the path of liberty for the Christian.

Dynamics of Contemplation:
On the Incarnation (#s 101-09)

The contemplation of the mysteries in the Exercises

From the beginning of the Second Week (#101) to the end of the Exercises the task of the exercitant is to obey the admonition that opens the book of the *Imitation of Christ*, which was so dear to Ignatius. "Let our primary study then be to meditate on the life of Jesus Christ. The doctrine of Christ surpasses all the doctrines of the saints; whoever has the Spirit will find therein a hidden manna" (I, 1-2).

Ignatius, therefore, exhorts us to let the life of Jesus be "our primary study," to find therein the hidden manna. On the first day of the Second Week he proposes to us somewhat diffusively the mysteries of the incarnation, annunciation and nativity. On the second day he wants us to meditate on the presentation of Jesus in the temple and the flight into Egypt. On the third day, Jesus in Nazareth and Jesus in the temple; the fourth day has a special meaning, as we shall see. From the fifth to the twelfth day he proposes the following meditations, which are to be repeated in five exercises: the baptism of Jesus in the Jordan; from the Jordan to the desert; the call of the disciples; the beatitudes; Jesus' appearance on the lake; Jesus preaching in the temple; the resurrection of Lazarus; the solemn entry into Jerusalem on Palm Sunday.

We have here fourteen meditations on the public life of Jesus; however, we are told that this is simply one possible selection, and hence we may add to or diminish this number. If one wishes to expand the list, Ignatius suggests in #162 the mystery of the visitation; the adoration of the shepherds; the circumcision; the visit of the Magi at Bethlehem. Thus, he opens the way to the contemplation of the entire life of Jesus, and in fact the appendix to the Exercises lists fifty mysteries (#s 261-312). For each one he indicates the three points to stress and the quotation of biblical passages that correspond to the various mysteries.

The abundance of all this material suggests to us that Ignatius considered the exercises as an apprenticeship to meditation and contemplation on the gospels, and he says as much explicitly in a note concluding the Second Week: "In fact, here we wish to offer only an indication and a method for contemplating better, or more systematically" (#162). Thus, the Exercises are also conceived of as an introduction to the *lectio divina,* that is, to a prayerful reading of holy scripture.

What is important in the contemplations of the exercitant? What does Ignatius stress as the main point, independently of the greater or smaller number of mysteries considered?

It is important, fundamental, that in every contemplation, starting with the first, we grow in affection for our Lord. To put this in more modern terms, we must seek to penetrate into the consciousness of Jesus, into his filial heart, to discover the manner in which he lived his messianic mission of salvation. The exercitant, therefore, must contemplate Jesus to become more like him, through an affective compenetration, born of love.

This is why he no longer speaks of meditations but rather of contemplations. Here the challenging proposal of following Jesus in humiliation, disregard and poverty (cf. #98) gives way to a tranquil identification of thoughts and actions with those of our Lord, so that we may fall in love with him, and so that it may be he himself who will free us, purify us, and transform us. And even if this proposal remains implicit in the dynamism of the various episodes, the purpose of the contemplation is to permit Jesus to shape our hearts as he wills and according to his mysterious ways, so that on our part we may not hamper his actions with rigid intellectual and deductive interventions.

Contemplation on the incarnation (#s 101-09)

I think it would be useful for us to briefly consider together the subject proposed for the first day:

"First contemplation: the incarnation. It includes the preparatory prayer, three preludes, three points and the colloquy" (#101).

This is no longer a meditation because, unlike what was called for in the First Week, we do not need to bring into play the faculties of memory, intellect, and will (remembering, reflecting, loving, willing and acting). The purpose is more directly contemplative, and hence we need to *see* the persons, *hear* their words, and *observe* their actions.

Ignatius is especially fond of simple outlines, which can help people to penetrate into the mystery, even if they are less experienced in the spiritual life and less cultured.

"The first prelude consists in calling to mind the subject of the contemplation: the three Divine Persons, observing the entire surface of the world filled with people and seeing all of them going to hell, resolve from all eternity that the Second Person become a man to save the human race; and thus, when the determined time had come, they sent the angel Gabriel to our Lady (cf. #262)" (#102).

In this #262 we find a more biblical explanation of the annunciation. The theological background, perhaps a rather elementary one which this prelude offers us, still shows the effort to penetrate into the mystery of Christ from a very ample point of view, which understands the incarnation as the determining event for the redemption of humanity.

"The second prelude is a mental representation of the place. We see the place; the huge extension of the world where so many and such diverse peoples live. We see in particular the house and the room of our Lady at Nazareth, in the province of Galilee" (#103). This attention to the place permits us to focus on the contrasts and to grasp the significance of this episode for humanity and for the divine plan of salvation.

"The third prelude consists in asking for what I want: this means asking for a more intimate knowledge of the Lord, who for my sake becomes a man, so that I may love him more and follow him" (#104).

And in #105 there is a remark that the request, the fruit to be obtained, will be the same for the whole week and for the following weeks as well. This clearly shows that the aim sought is a loving identification with Jesus, which leads to following him. "So that I may love him more and follow him." The end is always a choice according to God's plan for the salvation of my soul; a choice of being conformable to the Son, of being like him and in him through love, not simply through an exterior decision. If this affective, deep involvement springing from an intimate knowledge occurs, fellowship will be the almost spontaneous fruit of this assimilation to Christ.

I leave the reading of the three following points (#s 106-08) to you. In them, Ignatius seeks to bring into play the actions of the persons, what they say and do. He stresses however that all this too aims at making the exercitant enter, as it were, sensibly and personally, into the mystery.

Dynamics of contemplation

I prefer instead, to reply to the questions: What is, substantially, the dynamism of contemplation? What is the interior logic which brings about the transformation of the heart?

Here we need to repeat that this is not a deductive dynamism guided from without, but of itself it is entrusted to the power of the mystery, thanks to contact with the person of Jesus, with that of Mary, and with adoration of the Father who gives himself in his Son.

However, there is a certain logic which underlies that of the gospel, and which Ignatius recognizes as the logic of the incarnation. This comes out, for instance, in #s 108-09:

"I observe what people on earth are doing: They fight, they kill, they go to hell, and so on. I also observe the Divine Persons who accomplish the work of the sacred incarnation; furthermore I pay attention to what the angel and our Lady are doing: the angel fulfills his mission as a messenger, and our Lady, with an act of humility, thanks the divine Majesty. Finally, I reflect, seeking some fruit in each of these considerations" (#108). The fruit, as we said, is to know, love and follow Christ.

"Colloquy. I shall close the exercise with a colloquy, thinking of what I must say to the Divine Persons, or to the Incarnate Word, or to our Lady and Mother, according to what I feel in myself. I shall ask for help to follow and to imitate our Lord, as though he had just now become man" (#109), that is, in the very act of his self-giving.

In my opinion, what we have here is the dynamic of contrasts, which is typical of the mystery of the incarnation (we already saw this expressed in the previous meditation, in Philippians 2:5): the contrast between an unworthy world and a God who deigns to stoop to humanity; between a world of despair and a God who offers it hope looking upon us with mercy, compassion and goodness; between a work of cosmic and divine scope which concerns the entire universe, history and humanity, and the humility and insignificance of Nazareth, a tiny village in Galilee, and of Mary. It is the logic of contrast between God's greatness and the lowliness of the incarnation of the Word. And God thus abases himself *for me;* he is even now becoming incarnate *for me,* and out of love *for me* is traversing the way of deprivation and poverty to teach me how to return to him, how to re-discover sonship. Grasping the dynamism of God's merciful action, the exercitant comes to understand also the gospel dynamism and the manner of how he or she should live his or her own fellowship.

This logic is even more evident in the third point of the contemplation on the nativity:

As I behold the cave at Bethlehem, "I observe and consider what the persons are doing, for example, how they walk about and are concerned because the Lord is born in extreme poverty and will later die on the cross after having suffered so much from hunger, thirst, after insults and offenses of people—and all this for me" (#116). Beginning with the nativity we see the road toward Jerusalem, toward the cross; we see the choice of humility and poverty of the Word, incarnate for *me* so that by following his footsteps I, with him and in him, may find once more the glory of sonship.

Note that this is the same key for grasping the exercise given in the program of the king's call, but it helps to specify later on what it means to follow Jesus, to choose the beatitudes, to choose to go on to Jerusalem, there to be rejected like him, and to die like him for the love of my brethren.

I want to insist on the fact that this comes about without ideological imperatives or pedantic doctrinal assertions. It comes about instead by the force of the loving humanity of Jesus which is being contemplated, caressed as it were, loved, embraced, until it becomes part of our own mental outlook, which is identified with that of Jesus, according to the word of the apostle Paul, "The life I live now is not my own; Christ is living in me" (Gal 2:20).

Pastoral reflections

After trying to describe the dynamism of the Exercises of the Second Week, which are already presented in the first contemplation, let me set before you a pastoral reflection which I would state in the following terms.

The *lectio divina* presented in the Exercises is a prayerful reading of holy scripture, which tends to make us enter into the divine plan and is a gospel method for the transformation of the heart.

Thus, in the First Principle and Foundation Ignatius speaks of eliminating the disordinate affections, of making ourselves indifferent toward created realities, in such a way as to desire and choose only those which can best lead us to the end for which we were created (#21). The victory over hardness of heart and resistance to divine mercy, allowing ourselves to be fashioned by the Spirit of God, is fundamental in the Exercises.

However, although this victory is so important, once the First Week is over, Ignatius does not insist any more on direct purification of our disordinate affections, precisely because purification comes about through a transfiguration of the deep sentiments of a person's heart, through divine grace which flows from the filial humanity of Jesus.

For this reason, the *lectio divina* is the method for transforming the heart. Thanks to the affective contact, in the Spirit, with the humanity of Jesus, the exercitant subjects himself or herself to the Holy Spirit, who transfigures his or her existence into the image of the Son. Thus the Christian is formed to the likeness of Christ.

Today much is said about formation; but formation means precisely assimilating the Spirit of the Son, as revealed in his historical choices. They permit us to live a filial existence, even in a sinful, distorted, confused world, by reflecting in this human context the Spirit of Jesus.

The power of the *lectio divina* is therefore extraordinary, because it makes us accept the gospels as a concrete means to lead the life of sons and daughters of God in an unbelieving and sinful society.

Personal reflection

In conclusion, we may ask ourselves, how we can live this meditation and contemplation of the mysteries as we go through life?

I can distinguish three stages:

The first is the stage of childhood or spiritual adolescence. It is the simple acquaintanceship with the mysteries of Jesus we learn in Catholic youth groups, in study groups, by listening to sermons and catechism lessons. This is a most important acquaintanceship, a contact with the events of Jesus' life which is often decisive for the child or the growing youth. We must not underplay or consider as obvious this contact with the gospel stories in the catechism class, in sermons, in confession. We must not undervalue in our pastoral ministry the extraordinary impact of the first encounter with the absolute novelty of Christ, with his life from the crib to the cross, from Bethlehem to Nazareth and Jerusalem.

This is an encounter which can penetrate the heart, moving it and inflaming it; it is a great existential happening.

The second is the stage of growth toward Christian maturity, which we might call the moment of exegetical penetration, when one seeks to draw near to the gospel passage in all its richness, placing it in the context of holy scripture as a whole.

Ignatius remains, so to speak, between the first and the second stages: he starts the meditation on persons and events (#s 102-09), referring to the mysteries and giving gospel texts in the appendix (e.g., #262; Lk 1:26-38). He does so because in his day people could not dwell so deeply in the exegetical road, which is so characteristic of our modern times.

Today, thanks also to the Dogmatic Constitution *Dei Verbum* of Vatican II, all Christians are called to rediscover the exegetical tradition of the apostles, of Paul, and of the Fathers of the Church, so as to replace the events of Christ's life in the framework of the entire Bible.

Thus must we understand the *lectio divina* remembering for instance Paul who, without the help of concordances or computers, spoke to the early Christians about the mystery of Jesus with an extraordinary wealth of allusions to the Old Testament, that is, in the context of scripture as a whole.

The third phase which must be kept in mind all through the road of life is that of contemplative simplification. The passage and the event it relates enters into our hearts, into our daily actions, our great and small choices made according to Christ, and thus becomes the place where we habitually dwell.

This is a further, simpler stage of contact with the Word, not always realized as such, in which the facts of Christ's life nourish us in silence and we learn to enjoy them while keeping quiet.

Here again we find the power of the Ignatian Annotations, which at first glance may seem childish and obvious, but which in reality are loaded with this "dwelling in the event" thanks to the power of the words of the text. And thus we are nourished by holy scripture as by a manna which has no special taste because it has all of them together. We had, in fact, quoted at the beginning of this meditation the passage from the *Imitation*, "Let our primary study then be to meditate on the life of Jesus Christ. The doctrine of Christ surpasses all the doctrines of the saints; whoever has the Spirit will find therein a hidden manna," which alone can nourish our existence as Christians.

The Way of Humility

(Homily of Thursday after Ash Wednesday)

The way of the Messiah

"He said: 'The Son of man must suffer greatly and be rejected by the elders, the chief priests, and the scribes, and be killed, and on the third day be raised.'

"Then he said to all: 'If anyone wishes to come after me, he must deny himself and take up his cross daily and follow me. For whoever wishes to save his life will lose it, but whoever loses his life for my sake will save it. What profit is there for one to gain the whole world yet lose or forfeit himself? Whosoever is ashamed of me and of my words, the Son of man will be ashamed of when he comes in his glory and in the glory of the Father and of the holy angels. Truly I say to you, there are some standing here who will not taste death until they see the kingdom of God' " (Lk 9:22-25).

What is the context in which Jesus affirms: "The Son of man must suffer greatly"?

The context is the reply to the question about who Jesus is, a question which runs through the pages immediately preceding this gospel fragment, and which has its culminating point in the appeal made by Jesus to the disciples: "And you, who do you say that I am?" Peter's reply is pertinent: "You are the Christ of God" (Lk 9:18-21).

We might further explain this reply with the beautiful words of Paul VI, quoted in *Gaudium et Spes:* "The Lord is the goal of human history, the focal point of the desires of history and civilization, the center of humankind, the joy of all hearts, and the fulfillment of all aspirations" (#45). The meaning of Christ, Messiah, therefore, is precisely center of human history, the one who draws all things to himself, through whom all things must pass, and through whom all things find salvation.

It is not difficult to accept the centrality of Jesus in human history.

It is difficult, on the other hand, to accept the reply given by Jesus to Peter: The Christ of God, the Messiah, is indeed the center of history. But he chooses the path of humility, proclaims the beatitudes and expresses them in his own lowly life. He accepts the way of humility and fulfills it in his own life by being rejected by the elders, high priests and scribes, and by being put to death. This way of humility will shine forth in his resurrection on the third day.

This is the only way of the Messiah, and the only way for the filial transfiguration of humanity.

After specifying the historic nature of his messiahship, Jesus addresses not only his disciples but everyone: "If anyone wishes to come after me, he must deny himself and take up his cross daily and follow me."

This is the basic evangelical choice. To follow *this* Jesus, just as the gospels present him to us, the one in which we are called to make all other qualifying choices of life. As we have seen, the path of the Exercises seeks to lead us through love to a fundamental choice similar to that of Jesus, so that we may be able to rigthly carry out every great existential choice.

The only true way of life

Paraphrasing the first reading we can say that this is the only true way of life for humanity. Let us reread the text of Deuteronomy.

"Here, then, I have today set before you life and prosperity, death and doom. If you obey the commandments of the Lord your God, which I enjoin on you today, loving him and walking in his ways and keeping his commandments, statutes, and decrees, you will live and grow numerous and the Lord your God will bless you in the land you are entering to occupy. If, however, you turn away your hearts and will not listen but are led astray and adore and serve other gods, I tell you now that you will certainly perish; you will not have long life on the land which you are crossing the Jordan to enter and occupy. I call heaven and earth today to witness against you. I have set before you life and death, the blessing and the curse. Choose life, then, that you and your descendants may live, by loving the Lord your God, heeding his voice and holding fast to him. For that will mean life for you, a long life for you to live on the land which the Lord swore he would give to your fathers, Abraham, Isaac and Jacob" (Dt 30:15-20).

Let us translate this page in gospel terms. "I place before you life and good, death and evil, because today I command you to love the Lord your God, whose authentic countenance is revealed in his Son Jesus, and to walk in his ways observing his commandments, laws and norms. I command you to observe the beatitudes, the norms given in the Sermon on the Mount, so that you may live and multiply and thus the Church may come into being; and your God may bless you in the land which you are about to take possession of, and that thus the new Jerusalem may come into being, the new humanity." This is the way of life.

"But if your heart turns back, like those who, putting their hands to the plow, look behind them; if you do not listen, and instead prostrate yourself before possessions, ambitions and power, refusing the way of life, I declare to you today that you will perish, whoever you may be: Christians, Hebrews, Greeks, Muslims, Buddhists, etc. You will not have a long life and will enter the land of frustration, of despair and of trouble. As witnesses against you I take heaven and earth that I created for you so that you might be my sons and daughters and might possess the goods of the earth in the liberty of children. I have placed before you life and death in Jesus, that is, blessing and that curse which is the refusal of sonship. Choose life, then, so that you may live in the land which the Lord has sworn to give to your fathers Abraham, Isaac and Jacob—the land of eternal fullness."

The Two Positions in Contrast
(#s 136-46)

In a course of the Exercises as short as this one, it is necessary to leave to your own personal efforts the in-depth study of Ignatius' proposed contemplations. You can continue this effort even after this retreat, because the substance of what Ignatius suggested are the mysteries of the life of Jesus.

I would like, instead, to explain some key meditations, in particular those of the fourth day of the Second Week. These follow the two contemplations listed in #134: "Third day: Contemplate how Jesus at Nazareth was obedient to his parents, and *then* how they found him in the temple." Purposely, Ignatius inverted the order of the gospel accounts, because he takes them as symbols of the secular state in life (Jesus as obedient to his parents, and as a worker), and of the consecrated, religious state in life (Jesus separating himself from his parents to be busy with the things concerning his Father). We read, in fact, in #135: "We have considered the example that our Lord gave us for the ordinary state in life, which consists in observing the commandments, and for that of evangelical perfection; the first, when he obeyed his parents, the second, when he left his adoptive father and his earthly mother and remained in the temple to devote himself solely to the service of his eternal Father. Now we shall continue to contemplate the mysteries of his life, at the same time beginning to seek and to ask ourselves what is the state in life wherein the divine Majesty wishes us to serve him."

After a day spent on these two contemplations, the exercitant is considered ready to start the process of choice, of the election of his or her state in life, the nodal point of all the Exercises. For, "to order one's own life" according to God means, above all, to choose with rectitude the state in life corresponding with God's will. From the fourth day onward, everything aims at this, without however interrupting the meditation on the mysteries of the life of Jesus which serve as a backdrop to the search for the will of God. This search, for those who have already made a choice of a vocation, becomes a reform, that is, going back to one's original vocation.

Furthermore, #135 states: "As an introduction, in the first exercise that follows we shall consider what end Christ our Lord proposes to himself, and what end, on the contrary, the enemy of human nature has in mind. Then we shall see what our disposition must be to reach perfection in that state in life that God our Lord will propose that we embrace."

We have therefore two meditations here of a programmatic character, which aim at helping us realize both the subjective and the objective aspects of the choice of a way of life. The first is called "on two standards" (a contrast between Christ and the enemy of human nature) and the second is called "of the three classes of men" because it invites us to consider three different ways of reacting to the will of God.

I will stress the significance of the fourth day in the itinerary of the Exercises, offer some general observations on Christian existence as a continual struggle, reflect on the fundamental simplicity of the first meditation, and finally comment on the missionary mandate of Christ.

The fourth day (#136)

Let us begin with the title of the meditation.

"Meditation on two standards: one is Christ's, our sovereign leader and Lord; the other is Lucifer's, the mortal enemy of our human nature."

Immediately there follows the description of Christian life as a conflict, just as Ignatius conceived it to be.

The Christian life is not a simple, tranquil and progressive itinerary of assimilation to Christ, but rather a mortal conflict between two contradictory principles: one represented by Jesus, the principle of life, of sonship; the other personified in Lucifer, symbol of the principle of death and of the ruin of sonship.

We could just as well call #136 the meditation on two contrasting positions: life and death or progress and degradation of human existence, understanding them as a conflict between two powers. We do not have here two positions with various values involved; we have two positions expressing the law of contraries, as is clearly shown in #143. After the exercitant has been invited to imagine Lucifer who is plotting against humanity, we read: "On the other hand, we should imagine the supreme and true leader, who is Christ our Lord."

Existence as a conflict

The development of this first meditation (#s 137-46) is filled with biblical and patristic symbols, and obviously I cannot explain all the points in detail. I think it most important, however, to make a general observation on the concept of the Christian life as a conflict, precisely to evaluate the pastoral situation of our churches.

We often conceive the pastoral situation in a linear or

evolutive aspect: from bad to good, from good to better; or in its regressive aspect, from good to less good, to evil. And we complain when such positive development does not happen or appears slow and retarded. From this arises a sense of frustration, because we see with sorrow the decadence of faith, the drop in Sunday Mass attendance, and we mourn over the good old days.

We forget that Christian life is a constant struggle against the powerful influence of the idols, against Satan and his effort to bring people to incredulity and despair, to moral and physical suicide. We thus forget that the Christian's progress is to be measured not only by the length of the road travelled, but also by the number of obstacles overcome, of assaults withstood.

For this reason a judgment on the life of faith today appears to be very complex. It is not enough to evaluate the sociological indications, the number of people frequenting religious services, or the results of questionnaires concerning the importance given to the figure of Jesus compared with other figures—in other words, his ranking in a scale of values. A judgment on the life of faith must take into account the sometimes dramatic struggle for the faith and even for the gospel a Christian must engage in daily to continue believing and to make choices which correspond with gospel ideals, or at least to resist incredulity.

The meditation on two standards teaches us that the Lord sees his people in this light, and for this reason he has compassion on them, encourages them, upholds and consoles them. He is not a master who keeps an account of profits that increase or diminish; nor is he like a trainer who checks on the speed of his athletes and the records they have broken. Our Lord is a chief who encourages us in the battle, and who constantly heartens and reanimates us knowing full well how exhausting and difficult the struggle is, how astute and merciless our enemy.

Such an attitude, unfortunately too rare, may seem simplistic, but in reality it is very complex: in my opinion it
prevents many frustrations arising from a concept of the
pastoral task too much like that of a bookkeeper or a man-
ager; this latter seems to be one more influenced by ecclesiastical politics (keeping records of successes or failures)
than by a clear understanding of the true antagonistic nature
of the struggle for the kingdom of God.

We must, therefore, ask the Lord to give us this perception
which mitigates many anxieties about verifications which
are incapable of grasping the dramatic strife which being a
Christian is all about.

The two fundamental symbols (#s 140, 142, 315)

After the reflection inspired by attentive meditation on
this important page of the Exercises, important for its interpretation of the Christian's journey and that of the Church,
let us now take up the consideration of the two fundamental
symbols.

The negative symbol is set forth in #140: "Imagine a vast
open space in Babylon, and the leader of the adversaries who
is seated on a huge throne of fire and smoke, horrible and
terrifying to behold, and awe-inspiring."

Every detail in this description has a deep symbolical
value. First, the place: Babylon, the city of confusion, of
power, of opulence and of deception.

Then, the throne of the chieftain of the adversaries: this
throne in the original Spanish is *cátedra,* a great pulpit; this
indicates his pretension to know and to teach.

The fire and smoke stress the neurotic and unquiet confusion of this leader who seeks to impress us with his slogans
and catchwords.

"Horrible and terrifying," that is, one who creates fear,

fright, paralysis, anguish; who does not liberate, does not set free, but enchains the person.

Here we recognize the work of the negative spirit described more directly in the "Rules for the Discernment of Spirits," especially in the second and fundamental rule: "The evil spirit characteristically harasses, brings sadness, suggests difficulties, and, inspiring false reasoning, brings disquiet in order to prevent the soul from making any progress" (#315).

I must confess that sometimes when I listen to pastoral reflections or reports, I say to myself: are we not in the domain of remorse and sadness, accumulating difficulties, disturbances and false reasoning, where the only conclusion would be to stop and give up? Because, even though we claim to be lucid, sincere and honest in our investigations, in reality these efforts are not moved by the Spirit of God; they produce negativism, spite, bitterness, displeasure, fault-finding in ourselves and in others. The result of all this is frustration, or else indecision and fearfulness. If, in spite of it all one goes ahead, neglecting the analyses thanks to a certain determination, we still have to admit that we started on the wrong foot; we are not able to see and to grasp where and how the Spirit of God is at work, so we let ourselves be taken in by these negative and depressing suggestions of the spirit of evil.

The opposite symbol is given in #144:

"I shall consider Christ our Lord, in a vast, open meadow near Jerusalem, a beautiful, peaceful and humble spot."

The contrast with the description in #140 is obvious: Jerusalem; a beautiful, peaceful and humble spot; these are words which suggest to me openness, relaxation, the future (Jerusalem is the symbol of the future) and, at the same time, modesty, absence of pretensions, gentleness, peace and beauty. This is what is more explicitly described as the work of the Good Spirit in the second part of #135: "It is proper to the Good Spirit to give courage and energy, consolation and tears of joy, inspirations and serenity; it eliminates and removes all difficulties, so that one can go ahead in the way of good." As I said before, I sometimes feel that certain pastoral talks tend to increase the difficulties, not to remove them, so that one does not know what to do. The Good Spirit, on the other hand, gets to the heart of the problems, finds a way to resolve them, and helps us live out our faith.

At this point in our reflections we are invited to ask ourselves: What is my pastoral action like? Which of these two reactions do I provoke around me? More personally, what do I pay most attention to in my interior evaluations? in the evaluation of my existence? of the life of my church and of society?

Not that we need a naive optimism, because we have seen that the starting point is to recognize an exasperated and violent state of conflict. However, given that this state of conflict is due to opposing polarities, and that the Spirit of good has the upper hand, our analysis should take heart from the fact that today that Spirit is acting; we should seek his suggestions, look for the openings that he proposes, for the directions that he indicates, here and now, in this given situation of my life and of my church.

Christ's missionary mandate (#146)

Christ's program is laid down in #146: "I shall consider the discourse which Christ our Lord addresses to all his servants and friends, whom he sends on this mission. He is urging them to seek to help all by attracting them especially to great spiritual poverty and, if divine Majesty so wills and chooses to select them for it, to material poverty as well. Secondly, they should lead them to the desire of being humiliated and despised, for from these humility is born."

This missionary mandate of Jesus is particularly interesting. Strangely enough, Ignatius does not say: "Call the majority to the church, bring them to believe, have them come to Mass, baptize them." No, he says, "Help all without exception, liberate them, free them." Thus, in contrast with the program of Satan (cf. #142), who incites the demons to cast snares and chains before people, Jesus wants to liberate them from restraints, to loosen them from their chains, to help all to live an existence as authentic as his own, to live as free sons and daughters of the Father, despising the worldly slavery which binds people and makes them miserable and anguish-ridden.

I find it interesting to compare the mandate of Jesus with what we read in the gospel of Matthew: "Go, therefore, and make disciples of all nations, baptizing them in the name of the Father, and of the Son, and of the Holy Spirit, teaching them to observe all that I have commanded you. And behold, I am with you always until the end of the age" (28:19-20). In other words, make them live like me; make them live the Sermon on the Mount; teach them that true liberty of heart which all need—the baptized and the non-baptized, the practicing and the non-practicing, Jews, Muslims, Buddhists as well as atheists, agnostics, progressives, conservatives and the indifferent. Because all are called to enter into the liberty of Christ.

This is an extremely important aspect of our evangelizing mission, a kind of help that can be proposed to every person, regardless of his or her religious persuasion or faith. It does not consist in saying, above all, "Give up your convictions and take mine, which are better." It consists in offering help, stemming from the experience of Jesus, with which we all must compare ourselves if we wish to reach the liberty of sons and daughters.

This is, consequently, an aspect that cannot be absent from a balanced conception of missionary activity (even of the new evangelization). It means being capable of taking into consideration the finale of Mark's gospel: "Whoever believes and is baptized will be saved; whoever does not believe will be condemned" (16:16), as well as of the closing words of Matthew: "Go, therefore and make disciples of all nations, baptizing them in the name of the Father, and of the Son, and of the Holy Spirit, teaching them to observe all that I have commanded you. And behold, I am with you always until the end of the age" (28:19-20).

Yes, baptize them, make them share in God's sonship, but in order that they may live a new life as disciples, following the Sermon on the Mount.

Today, in fact, in many situations in Europe and especially in Asia, the aspect of discipleship according to the Sermon on the Mount seems to be more readily acceptable than that which speaks of baptism, and we have to realize this so as not to make of our new evangelization a simple matter of confessional proselytism, which goes against the grain and hence is going to be refused. To those who assert that they already have their own religious convictions or that they are atheists, we can simply say: "But you are not truly free interiorly; you suffer anguish, you have not found peace, and thus there is still a stretch of road to be pursued, even for you."

All people, I repeat, feel the need of the liberty taught by Jesus, even if they already have a faith to which they adhere. They want to be freed of their anguish, they want to find peace. It is this road to peace which we must propose in an ethical, practical way of life, which will bring people to get rid of the many daily harassments of modern life.

I am convinced that our capacity of discerning this aspect for our engagement in the new evangelization, will bring about in many the acceptance of the proposal of a filial life according to the gospel.

Conclusion

The first meditation of the fourth day, which has suggested to us some important points of reference for our life as Christians and as pastors, closes with a triple colloquy.

"First, I shall address a colloquy to our Lady so that she may obtain from her Son our Lord the grace of my being accepted under his standard, especially in total poverty of spirit, and, if the divine Majesty wills it so and is willing to choose and welcome me, even in material poverty. I will ask her to obtain the grace of enduring humiliations and insults so as to imitate Christ better, provided I endure them without any sin on the part of anyone and without any offence to the divine Majesty" (#147). The second and the third colloquies ask the same grace of the Son and of the Father.

In our personal meditation we can repeat this prayer slowly, asking ourselves: What does this mean to me? Am I making any progress toward what Ignatius wishes to obtain? The reply will also be useful to help me understand the profound value of the missionary mandate of Jesus which I have chosen to follow.

An Authentic
Christian Humanism

Although we are already at the last day of our Exercises, we have barely sketched the long road of one who follows Jesus in an affective assimilation of his public life. We still need to speak about the preliminaries for the choice of a way of life (#s 149-68) and about the process of choosing itself, which begins at #169. After this we find two more weeks in Ignatius' book. In these the choice is interiorized and confirmed through meditating on the passion and the resurrection of Jesus. Thus, the outlook is vast indeed.

However, since the time for our spiritual retreat is almost over, I think it would be useful to answer at least three questions regarding certain pages of the Exercises, which we have not had an opportunity to comment on, in the desire of giving greater organic appeal to the preceding reflections.

— What is it that underlies the "choice of a state in life"? How can this attitude, which seems to be necessary only once in a lifetime, instead be important through our entire Christian journey? The reference is especially to #189 of the Exercises and to #230, where Ignatius sets before us that meditation which sums up everything and concludes all: the "contemplation to attain love."

— How do the actual choices of Christ influence our individual choices?

— Finally, what is the sufficient attitude and what is the optimum attitude which will enable us to make truly free qualifying choices? To answer this last question, I shall examine #s 165-68.

The pathway of interior liberty (#s 175-88 and 230-37)

What underlies the "choice of a state in life"?

The attitude which the Exercises seek to promote in order to permit a correct choice of a state in life is interior liberty. This is furthermore sought as a permanent condition which will insure that every decision regarding the kingdom of God is made in true freedom of heart.

For this precise reason Ignatius proposes certain exercises aimed at reforming one's daily life to whoever cannot or does not need to make a choice of a state in life. He keeps in mind each person's profession, so that everything may be governed by truly evangelical choices. We read in #189: "To amend and reform one's state in life. A warning for those who are bound to an ecclesiastical office or may be married, whether they have many earthly goods or very few. They may not want or be able to make a choice in those things which are subject to change. It will be of much help to offer them, instead of a choice, a method for improving and reforming their present state in life, by directing their existence and their state to the greater glory of God our Lord and the salvation of their souls. To achieve this end, whoever is in such a situation must consider at length—through the Exercises and the manner of making the choice already explained in #s 175-88—what sort of house and retinue of servants to have, how to direct and govern it, and how to educate therein by both word and deed. He or she should act in the same way regarding how much to set aside for family and household needs, and how much to give to the poor or to other pious works, without willing or seeking, in all and for all, anything but the greater praise and glory of God our Lord. We should all realize that we progress in the spiritual life in proportion to how much we liberate ourselves from self-love, from our own will, and from our own interests."

Hence, the attitude of liberty, required for the choice of a state in life, is necessary even in our small, daily choices. What counts is to have ascertained, at least once in a lifetime, the possibility, the conditions, and the road leading to real interior liberty, as the pre-condition for allowing oneself to be guided by the Spirit in every evangelical choice.

We understand better how the dynamics of the Exercises aim at being an education in Christian liberty, which will help us to always choose what is pleasing to God, without any attachments, impediments or prejudices, without any personal preferences.

We find the same idea stressed in #s 230-37 at the end of the Fourth Week, under the title of the "contemplation for attaining love."

Ignatius proposes a very simple exercise, one applicable for one's whole life, which imposes on the exercitant a eucharistic attitude in every occasion of the day. This is an attitude of thanksgiving and praise, of offering our own selves, with all that we do and experience, to God. Such an attitude is realizable only when the heart has already liberated itself from worldly conditioning. It is not enough to discover this attitude, to recognize its beauty, and to call it to mind from time to time. What is needed is to have a free heart, and in this sense the contemplation for attaining love is the fruit of the entire journey of the Exercises. Thus, freed from the earthly ties that bind and hinder us, having attained filial liberty in Christ, and having identified ourselves as far as possible in his conscience, we shall, like Jesus, have eyes and hearts wide open to the praise of God at every moment, capable of seeing God's action in the joyful or sorrowful events of our existence. And to this God who loves us, who gives himself to us, who is present in every detail of our lives, let us respond with a eucharistic offering which takes in our whole existence and is expressed in this well-known prayer:

> Take, O Lord,
> and receive all my liberty,
> my memory, my understanding and my will;
> all that I have and possess you have given to me;
> and to you I give it all back.
> It is all yours;
> dispose of it according to your will.
> Give me only your love and your grace;
> this alone suffices for me. (#234)

I remember something which touched me deeply. One day last year, I went to visit a young priest who, after having endured a painful illness, was now in the final state of his agony. Serenely he looked at me and said these simple words: "Take and receive, O Lord!" He then added that it was very, very hard for him to say those words but that he wanted to keep on saying them. He died two days later, and I learned that the year before he had made a thirty-day retreat on the Ignatian model. His "take and receive" was really a eucharistic offering, a sacrifice of his entire existence.

An authentic Christian humanism

What part do the actual choices of Christ play in our individual choices?

The question is important because, in a rather rigid understanding of the Exercises, one might think that the choices of Christ (contemplated in the meditation on his life, passion, death and resurrection) become ours in a somewhat automatic and deductive way and end up conditioning the choices of the exercitant. In such a scenario, the Exercises would lead to a form of impoverishment, limiting us to Jesus' choices of poverty and humility. How can those who do not leave everything, who marry or dedicate themselves in their professions, obey Christ's choices of poverty and humility, so starkly presented by Ignatius from the Second Week on?

We need to clear up this point definitely.

If we read the book we notice that the demanding proposals do appear in the decisive moments *prior* to the choice but are no longer mentioned in the process of the choice itself.

The difference is very significant; something Ignatius carefully pondered. When one makes a choice, the reference is to the general principles dealing with God's glory and the salvation of one's soul, not to the concrete and historic choices made by Christ. Since these latter are obviously not meant for all, they could predetermine the exercitant's choice, thus preventing a true search into all the possibilities God offers.

Let us compare two pages of the Exercises.

"I shall address a colloquy to our Lady so that she may obtain from her Son our Lord the grace of my being accepted under his standard, especially in total poverty of spirit, and, if the divine Majesty wills it so and is willing to choose and welcome me, even in material poverty. I will ask her to obtain the grace of enduring humiliations and insults so as to imitate Christ better, provided I endure them without any sin on the part of anyone and without any offence to the divine Majesty" (#147).

This colloquy is proposed for the fourth day of the Second Week, at the end of the meditation on the two standards.

When it comes to proceeding with the choice such language is not found again. Let us now reread #177, where the third time in which a choice should be made is described. "The third period is a period of tranquillity, when we consider above all the end for which we were born, namely, to praise God our Lord and to save our souls. Consequently, desiring this end, I shall choose as the means a state in life among those approved by the Church, so that I may be helped in serving the Lord and saving my own soul. 'Period of tranquillity' is understood as a time in which the soul is not agitated by various spirits, and exercises its natural faculties freely and quietly."

Again, in #179, where Ignatius speaks of the various elements of making a good choice, he does not tell us to keep in mind the choices made by Christ, but "the end for which I was created, which is to praise God our Lord and save my soul; and at the same time I must remain indifferent, without any disordinate affections, so that I may not be inclined or eager to accept the thing proposed rather than to refuse it, or to refuse it rather than to accept it. Rather, I must keep myself in balance, like the weight on the lance of a scale, ready to perform what I shall judge most useful for the glory and praise of God our Lord, and for the salvation of my soul."

So, in the time preceding the choice we are drawn to the choices of Christ; but at the moment of making our choice we must remain completely free in the face of the whole range of human possibilities.

After noting this important difference, there may arise another question: What becomes of Jesus' choice of poverty and humility, if such values do not come into play at the decisive moment?

We can find the answer in various places in the Exercises. I shall limit myself to recalling #155, in the course of the meditation on the three classes of people who must make a choice. Of these three groups or classes of people the one who reaches the perfect disposition for making a choice is not the one who automatically opts for poverty and for giving up money, but the one who chooses interior detachment from it. "The third person wishes to do away with the affection [for money] and at the same time wishes to remain indifferent with regard to it. This person wants to keep it or not keep it according to what God our Lord may inspire and what he or she will judge as being most useful for the service and praise of the divine Majesty. In the meantime, he or she is completely detached and strives not to want the money nor any other thing, unless so urged by the service of our Lord. Thus, it will be the desire to serve God our Lord better which will be the determining factor to take or to leave money."

The key word here is "completely detached" which in the Spanish original is more meaningful and might be better translated by the expression "affectively abandons what he or she has." An affective detachment, then, which may or may not lead to an effective detachment, depending on the general circumstances in which the will and the glory of God will be best brought about.

We can conclude by affirming that our assimilation to Christ, our being with Jesus, is accomplished above all and principally in the heart, not in a mechanical imitation which does not correspond with the richness and the variety of God's plans for humanity. Ignatius has succeeded in joining the deepest desire to imitate Jesus the poor, humble and despised, with an authentic and total liberty of choice among the various manners of serving God. While insisting on the poverty and the humility of Jesus, he is not an advocate of beggary but a genuine promoter of Christian liberty. He aims at the organic construction of a new humanity in all its forms, whether by renunciation or by the legitimate use of earthly goods.

For this reason we can say that Ignatius has promoted an authentic Christian humanism, which is not simply a choice in favor of humanity but rather for the man Jesus Christ. Christians are those who want only and absolutely Jesus, with all their hearts, with all their minds and all their strength; all the rest they want or choose in subordination to him.

Such is the dynamism according to which the choices of Christ come into play in our individual choices; a dynamism reaching its high point in our hearts, in our affections, in the fullness of our dedication which liberates the heart and disposes it to seek what will best contribute to the glory and honor of God.

The sufficient attitude and the optimum attitude for a free choice (#s 165-68)

Finally, we need to reply to the third question: What is the attitude which is sufficient, and what is the attitude which is best, in order to accomplish a free choice?

To answer this it would be well to go back to #s 165-68 of the book, which brings before us, even before the process of a real and true choice, the so-called three degrees of humility. These are a series of attitudes, some sufficient, others better, and the last best of all. They are three degrees of humility, love, or availability, corresponding to three ways of progressively preparing oneself for making a good choice, for making free choices throughout one's life. These are the transposition, in view of the choice, of the three graces of purification on which we reflected during the meditation on sin. It may be of help to reread them in #63:

"The first colloquy is with our Lady, so that she may obtain for me from her Son three graces: the first that I may acquire an intimate knowledge and detestation of my sins; the second, that I may realize the disorder in my actions and, detesting them, bring order into my life; the third, that I may come to know the world and thus, detesting it, may keep myself far from earthly vanities."

We said that these three graces or attitudes are basic through the entire path of purification. In my opinion, they reappear in the book under the title "the three degrees of humility."

To the first grace—the knowledge and detestation of my sins—corresponds the first degree of the right disposition for choosing, as described in #165.

"The first degree of humility is necessary for eternal salvation. It consists in abasing and humbling myself as much as I can to obey in all things the law of God our Lord, so that I may never decide to transgress any divine or human commandment that binds me under the pain of mortal sin, even if I were to become the lord of all earthly riches, or to save my earthly life."

Here we have a good and fundamental disposition, necessary for every existential choice: never to choose to commit a mortal sin.

To the second grace—knowledge and detestation of the disorders of my life—corresponds the second degree of proper disposition for making a choice, explained in #166: "The second degree of humility is more perfect than the first. It consists in being disposed neither to desire nor to have wealth rather than poverty; to seek honors rather than dishonor; to desire a long life rather than a short life; provided that the service of God our Lord and the salvation of my soul will be equally well served. Besides this indifference, it also supposes that I may never decide to commit a venial sin, not for all the riches in the world, nor to save my life."

This degree of availability insures a correct choice. The

reference here is not only to choices which avoid what is forbidden but also to so many other choices of this life. Be it in the professional world or in serving others, the motive must not be our own interest or profit, even if legitimate, but rather the glory of God.

Is there an even more secure disposition, which allows us to better overcome the uncertainties and the torpor of the human heart?

Ignatius replies affirmatively and wants us to obtain this by asking for it as earnestly as possible in prayer, because this is a gift of God, not a result of human efforts.

To this third grace—knowledge and detestation of the world's vanities—we can, therefore, connect this best disposition, the most perfect one, toward which we have been incited ever since the meditation on the king's call (#98) and which is described in #167:

"To imitate Christ our Lord more concretely and to be like him, I want and I choose poverty with Christ, the poor one, rather than wealth; humiliations with Christ, the humbled one, rather than honors; furthermore, I prefer to be considered a fool for Christ, who was first so considered, rather than wise and clever according to the world's judgments."

Only this choice truly establishes us in the full dynamism of the gospel. Jesus strives in every way to lead Peter and the other disciples to this attitude, beginning with the revelation in Caesarea all the way to his death; but they will reach it only after the resurrection, through the grace of the Holy Spirit.

Not by chance does Ignatius note: whoever desires this third degree of humility must pray much, "beseeching our Lord to be chosen for this greater and more perfect humility, in order to imitate and serve him better, provided that there be equal or greater service and praise to the divine Majesty" (#168).

It is only with this choice that the Church grows in true holiness. It is only with this kind of availability that pastoral actions are incisive and authentic. It is only in this atmosphere of love that saints can flourish, that the government of the Church is truly spiritual, apostolic and free, and that the kingdom of God comes with power.

In conclusion, we can say that the holy eucharist contains in itself the choices of Christ, makes them actual, represents them every day, and hence forms and renews them in us. And our ministry, which is above all at the service of the holy eucharist, is at the service of those choices.

Let us invoke the Holy Spirit for one another, asking him to place us, thus, in the very heart of Christ.

Expressing the Gospel
in Our Surroundings

(Homily for Friday after Ash Wednesday)

An example of prophetic denunciation

The first reading, taken from the book of the prophet Isaiah, is an example of prophetic denunciation.

"Cry out full-throated and unsparingly; lift up your voice like a trumpet blast; tell my people their wickedness and the house of Jacob their sins. They seek me day after day and desire to know my ways, like a nation that has done what is just, and not abandoned the law of their God. They ask me to declare what is due them, pleased to gain access to God.

"Why do we fast, and you do not see it? Afflict ourselves, and you take no note of it?

"Lo! on your fast day you carry out your own pursuits and drive all your laborers. Yes, your fast ends in quarreling and fighting, striking with wicked claw. Would that today you might fast so as to make your voice heard on high! Is this the manner of fasting I wish, of keeping a day of penance, that a man bow his head like a reed and lie in sackcloth and ashes? Do you call this a fast, a day acceptable to the Lord?

"This, rather, is the fasting that I wish, releasing those bound unjustly, untying the thongs of the yoke; setting free the oppressed breaking every yoke; sharing your bread with the hungry, sheltering the oppressed and the homeless, clothing the naked when you see them, and not turning your back on your own. Then shall your light break forth like the dawn, and your wound shall quickly be healed; your vindication shall go before you and the glory of the Lord shall be your rear guard. Then shall you call, and the Lord will answer; you shall cry for help, and he will say, 'Here I am!' " (Is 58:1-9).

Authentic religiosity and love of neighbor

The crimes and sins of the people against which the prophet is invited by God to cry out, do not consist in wicked actions spectacularly new or heinous, but in the contrast between their apparent religiosity and the daily injustice that fills their lives.

There is an external religiosity ("They seek me day after day and desire to know my ways") which is contrasted with the people's everyday lives ("You carry out your own pursuits and drive all your laborers. Yes, your fast ends in quarreling and fighting, striking with wicked claw"). The text does not speak of murders or civil wars but rather of those daily disputes over practical matters, which cannot co-exist with true seeking of the Lord.

Our attention is called to Isaiah's denunciation, because it thus gives us a measuring-rod and a sign by which to judge authentic religiosity, which shows itself in real love of neighbor.

Naturally, religion is not exhausted with love of neighbor alone; it is necessary to seek God, to long to know his ways, to live in a personal relationship with him; however, the concrete sign in everyday living is love of neighbor in all its forms: "setting free the oppressed . . . clothing the naked . . ."

From this profound religiosity—this sense of the Lord's nearness which is expressed in love of neighbor—there comes the promise of a spiritual rebirth of community, and we might even say, a spiritual rebirth of the Church. "Then shall your light break forth . . . the Lord will answer . . . 'Here I am.' "

At first glance, it would seem that the prophet's admonitions do not have much connection with the series of the

Exercises which we are about to complete. And why is it that in the Exercises we find no word about love of neighbor? about solidarity? The answer is easy. Above all we sought to contemplate Jesus Christ; he is the gospel and to be in him is to be in the gospel. Living divine love as a consequence of right evangelization means, in the first place, to be like Jesus, a son in the Son. It means sharing in his filial trust, living out our call as sons and daughters of the Father, giving ourselves completely to him, choosing him alone.

Only through such participation in the sonship of Jesus can we also share in his love for humanity. By remaining in him we come to participate in the wealth of his love poured out upon people. Christ is the source of all real manifestations of divine love. And in these days of retreat we wish precisely to draw closer to that source, to enter into the eucharistic heart of Jesus, so as to draw from that torrent of love poured out on all humanity. In this way we fully live the gift of our episcopacy, the gift of consecrating all our time and all our energies to the service of others, of putting our lives at the disposal of a gospel which is expressed concretely in our daily actions, in our continual and incessant acts of love of neighbor.

Lord Jesus, we thank you for the gift of being called to inevitable love of neighbor, which we cannot escape, because it invades our heart and thoughts. May we always slake our thirst at the fountain of love which you are and nourish ourselves by your eucharist, which signifies total dedication to the Father and devotedness to our brothers and sisters. We thank you for having called us to share in your mystery of the Son from which this closeness derives. And we want to ask you to give a new outpouring of your Spirit of love, so that in our dioceses we may always bear witness to the openness of God's mystery in earthly realities, and from earthly realities to the mystery of the Trinity.